GAMES
LOVERS
PLAY

GAMES LOVERS PLAY

Breaking Through
to an Honest Relationship

E. Edward Reitman, Ph.D.

WILLIAM MORROW AND COMPANY, INC.
NEW YORK 1984

ACKNOWLEDGMENTS

I have always wanted to write a book. I wanted to be able to share my thoughts, feelings, and love with more than just the people immediately around me. But I was never sure I could do it. It took the assistance and encouragement of some very special people to make that wish come true. From the start my wife, Harriet, had no doubt that it would come about. To that end she gave up many of our Saturdays and evenings together and provided her honest criticism, always wanted but not always palatable.

Then there was Joan Eggleston who was there from the start, pushing me to clarify my ideas and sharing all the ups and downs. Sharon Dotson helped so very much when it came time to provide a professional touch to some of the material. Barbara Merryman typed many an evening away. Rosemary Blincow did the same and, in addition, she and Linda Bailey greatly helped to make order out of the paper work that streamed from my office. There is no way to truly express my appreciation to Elizabeth Frost Knappman, a very special long-distance friend, who not only lent her sensitivity, encouragement, and technical skills to me and the manuscript but who always seemed to say just what I needed at the right time. Last there are my patients who, over the years, have stimulated my mind, shared with me a special kind of closeness, and provided much of the material in this book.

To all of them I am deeply indebted for their involvement, their encouragement, and most of all, the love we shared during this project.

—EER

CONTENTS

PART I
LOVE IS AN ILLUSION

PART II
REAL LOVING IS POSSIBLE

To love at all is to be vulnerable. Love anything and your heart will certainly be wrung and possibly be broken. If you want to make sure of keeping it intact, you must give your heart to no one, not even to an animal. Wrap it carefully round with hobbies and little luxuries; avoid all entanglements; lock it up safe in the casket or coffin of your selfishness. But in that casket—safe, dark, motionless, airless—it will change. It will not be broken; it will become unbreakable, impenetrable, irredeemable. The alternative to tragedy, or at least to the risk of tragedy, is damnation. The only place outside Heaven where you can be perfectly safe from all the dangers of love is Hell.

—C. S. LEWIS

PART I
Love Is
an Illusion

CHAPTER 1

Deceptive Love: Losing When You Win

All of us have known "love." It's a word we grew up with, have heard in countless songs, have seen on television, and have read about in magazines. For some, love cures all ills, conquers all obstacles, tames the heart of the wildest beast. For others, love means caring for someone else more than yourself. Whatever the definition, most of us feel life is incomplete without love.

But something is wrong with these notions. What's wrong is that they assume that loving is a *natural* human activity.

But, if love is so natural, why are there so many divorces? And why are so many people attending marriage encounter groups or church-sponsored events for singles. Why are they reading the latest books that guarantee they'll find an intimate relationship? Love doesn't come easily, and it isn't commonplace.

Still, people want to love and be loved. If they can get that feeling from a spouse, a friend, a child, or a parent, then they have a sense of well-being that surpasses the satisfaction of a new car or house, or this year's promotion. And yet, as a psychologist, I have a tremendously busy schedule filled with people who say to me, "I love this person, yet I feel so empty inside. I don't know why my relationship isn't any good, but I've got to get out or I'll go crazy."

And I respond, "What happened to that wonderful experience you had when you fell in love? What do you want from this relationship?"

They invariably answer, "Caring, sharing, being able to disclose myself to someone else. Wanting to do for somebody else as much as I would like done for me. Being able to say to someone, 'Here I am. Can you accept me, can you love me with all my insufficiencies and fears?' "

It sounds good, but if we want that kind of love, and if loving is natural, why aren't we all natural-born lovers? How come love doesn't come easily for you and me in the relationships we are already in? Why are people who claim they know exactly what they want unable to achieve it with the people they love? The answer is simple.

There is a radical difference between love in the mind and the heart and love as we experience it. The latter I call pragmatic love. That kind of love is the reliving, again and again, of so-called loving behavior we experienced as children. To love with our childhood misconceptions is to seek relationships that die when the sugar coating is gone. Such love results in considerable unhappiness in the long run. Unfortunately, it is the way most of us try to give and get love.

In the name of that kind of love, people cheat on one another, punish one another, deceive one another. We start the process early. Boys have to impress their dates; girls go farther sexually than they really wish. Men have to perform in the work world and in bed in order to deserve love. Women bow to chauvinistic lovers who resent careers and forget that some women have two full-time jobs: their careers and their homes.

There are many people who stay together, whether they are married or not, and who have relationships built on tenuous foundations. When you ask them why they live like that, the answer, you guessed it, is "I love that person."

But is love submitting to an insensitive lover? Is real love performing, trying to impress? No. Still, this is what many people affirm by their behavior. Love, apparently, is not that beautiful, natural behavior we think it is. Mankind conceived an ideal of love that we claim to believe, but it's amazing how many of us, despite our intellectual and emotional concurrence—our compatibility—behave hypocritically.

For instance, Elizabeth tells me she believes that love is the freedom to be yourself, but in practice, her loving endeavors consist of allowing others to dominate her life. Her parents told her, "We'll send you to college on the condition that you take the courses we think best for you."

What they thought best for her was a teaching certificate, because it would lead to a job. All through school Elizabeth kept saying, "I'd like to take business courses, or go to law school," to which her parents replied, "If you want our help, be a teacher."

Throughout her life, Elizabeth got what she wanted by acquiescing to her parents. When she married, her successive husbands treated her much as her parents did, and she behaved in the same way. If she was compliant, and if she did what she did not want to do, she got support and love.

In each of her three marriages, she was the same obedient, submissive person. This aided her in getting what she perceived as love, because love, to Elizabeth, is being the victim. It may be a negative experience, but it is involvement.

Meredith equates love with money, not necessarily dollar bills, but tangible things. She'll tell you she believes that real love is having someone take care of you, but she evaluates whether a man loves her or not by how much the meal costs when he takes her out. If he takes her to Antoine's, he must really like her. If he takes her to McDonald's, she must not rate. As a child, her parents bestowed love by giving gifts. The bigger the gift, the more they loved her.

Finally there is Max, a handsome, well-educated man with a great job. Max's mom wasn't very demonstrative. So to get attention Max became a most obnoxious teenager. At home he sassed his parents and refused to cooperate with other family members on even the simplest matters. At school he was the boy who shot spit balls secretly from the back of the room and made crude remarks to the good-looking girls in the class. Now, years later, every time he is faced with a potential relationship, Max becomes unbearable.

What kind of loving will each of you seek? It will be the same kind of love that you got from your parents. You will respond just as you did as a child. We may all know that love is not being manipulated, not having money spent on us, or not taking care of the world's hapless, but each of us uses these or some other learned behavior that masquerades as love in our day-to-day lives.

How can we recognize these behaviors in our loving interactions? We all have our own early loving experiences to draw on, but here is a test that will indicate to what degree you engage in fraudulent loving, that is, persisting to love the way you did as a child rather than risking openness, honesty and vulnerability. As you take this test remember that none of us altogether escapes the affliction of fraudulent love. Somewhere in this test you will find yourself. The question is, to what degree are we guilty of loving dishonestly?

Are You a Fraudulent Lover?

Take This Test and Score Your Ability to Love Openly

On the following ten multiple choice questions, each answer is worth between one and five points. Use this table to determine your response.

1 Point	Never
2 Points	Rarely
3 Points	Sometimes
4 Points	Frequently
5 Points	Always

1. Are You Insecure and (a) defer to your lover's every wish_____, (b) seek their constant approval_____, (c) fear he/she will leave you_____, (d) avoid saying what you think_____?

2. Do You Buy Love and (a) do you do what you really don't want_____, (b) do more for someone else than he/she can possibly do in return_____, (c) embarrass friends with extravagant gifts_____,(d) agree with others rather than voice your own opinion_____?

3. Are You Jealous and (a) bristle if your lover hugs or touches someone else_____, (b) feel ignored if your spouse or mate indulges in a long conversation with a member of the opposite sex_____, (c) resent your lover's friends of the same or opposite sex_____, (d) even resent your mate interacting with his or her own family members_____?

15

4. Do You Pout and (a) use the silent treatment if you are crossed_____, (b) become sullen when you disapprove of your mate's words or actions_____, (c) retreat from physical contact when your feelings are hurt_____, (d) refuse to join in potentially enjoyable activities in an effort to create guilt in others_____?

5. Is Sex Dissatisfying (a) to the point that you feel used when having intercourse_____, (b) to the point that you agree to have sex when you don't want to_____, (c) and causes you to have problems when performing sexually_____, (d) and you find it difficult to ask for what you like_____?

6. Are You Manipulative and (a) hide financial matters, the children's problems, and other personal difficulties from your spouse_____, (b) use physical force as a means of getting your own way_____, (c) get depressed when your mate doesn't do what you want_____, (d) believe that what your partner doesn't know won't hurt him or her_____?

7. Do You Harbor Resentments (a) like forever nagging your mate about inconsequential behaviors such as forgetting to turn off the lights, picking up clothes, and putting the cap on the toothpaste _____, (b) by holding on to angry feelings long after the conflict itself is forgotten_____, (c) finding yourself annoyed and embarrassed by the way your lover behaves in public or at social engagements _____, (d) and feeling the need to get even_____?

8. Do You Keep Score and (a) ruminate on and finally drag out all past wrongs, thus keeping yourself depressed and dissatisfied_____, (b) keep a list of old transgressions that you pull out to stifle your partner whenever you argue or disagree_____, (c) harbor one old stand-by resentment that you can, "never forgive him for"_____, (d) even when he or she is really trying, do you give up and say "he or she can never change"_____?

9. Are You Controlling and (a) do you threaten divorce_____, (b) have you ever physically abused or hit and pushed your mate_____, (c) do you demand to make the ultimate decision on important issues_____, (d) do you insist on having the last word_____?

10. Are You Remote and (a) do you feel isolated and unneeded when your partner is successful_____, (b) do you feel strong and essential when your partner is feeling weak_____, (c) do you find work to do or become sleepy when there is a real opportunity for togetherness_____, (d) do you invite others to come along when the two of you go out_____?

The highest possible score for this test is 100 points. The lowest possible score is 20. Determine your score by adding up the total of all your answers and dividing by 2; then, interpret your test profile in terms of the following three categories:

0–33: This is a surprisingly low score. If valid, it suggests an unusually open, straightforward means of communicating with your mate. You are to be complimented.

34–66: Most of us probably fall into this category. To some extent, we experience insecurities and fears that interfere with our ability to love honestly. This test can highlight a particular area where we experience the most difficulty.

67–100: Despite being on the upper end of the scale, this range of scores suggests early emotional hurts that now make it difficult for you to love openly, or to risk rejection and confrontation with someone you love. On the positive side, this range also suggests some degree of honesty and indicates a strong willingness to look at yourself and grow.

After taking this revealing test, try another approach. Take the test for your mate; then have your mate take the test for you. If you have no spouse or lover, have someone you trust and whom you feel knows you take the test as though they were you. The resulting score could provide you with an intriguing comparison between how another sees you contrasted with your own profile.

Keep your score handy. After you've finished reading this book and applied some of the suggestions, go back and take the test again. A comparison of the two scores will show that you are loving more openly.

If all of us are fraudulent lovers to some degree, how do we eliminate such unrewarding behavior? We need to find new ways to deal with the people whom we want to be close to, or we'll never be happy in love.

Yet people rarely change. Those early messages we received in childhood never alter. So our basic methods of getting and giving love never leave us until the day we die.

I grew up in a large family in which I was the first grand-child. Everyone constantly told me how great I was, including my mother. But Mom was so insecure that she herself was never happy. She got love by feeling depressed. And every time she felt bad, it seemed as if it was my job to make her feel better.

And so that's how I've lived my life. That's partly why I became a psychologist. I can get a lot of love by helping people feel happier. My mother encouraged me to do that, to the extent that if she walked into the room today and looked unhappy, I would feel this terrible feeling inside and think, "What can I possibly do to make her feel good?" But there was nothing I could *ever* do in my whole life to make her feel any better. I could give you dozens of examples.

Whenever she came to visit—for a bar mitzvah or a wedding—my wife, Harriet, and I would take Mom to the beauty parlor to have Mom's hair done. On the way back home Mom would inevitably say, "Did you see that lady in the other chair?"

I'd answer, "No, I didn't see that lady in the other chair."

"Well, she got the hairdo that I like. The girl you gave me to didn't do it right."

And that evening, before we went out, we'd find her in the bathroom combing out what we had tried to give her and restoring the usual bun on the top of her head. So even though I was the greatest son in the world, she made sure I didn't feel too great.

Today, when I go home and my wife doesn't look happy, I get anxious. That underlying attitude will never change for me, ever, for the rest of my life. This expression of love was ingrained in me.

A WAY TO CHANGE

There is a solution. It's a new way of viewing change, and I think it's the only solution life experiences can provide us.

In growing up we learned a repertoire of, say, five ways to deal with feeling unloved and for obtaining the love we need. Let's say they included being good, being submissive, or possibly rebelling, fighting, or running away. Perhaps out of the five behaviors, one is healthy. The others are nonproductive, or even downright destructive. That means 80 percent of the time we are behaving in a way that's destructive and feeling rotten about ourselves because of it.

We can't change these behaviors. Life doesn't give us an eraser, either. We try to forget, to put things in the back of our minds to avoid thinking about them. We try to be so busy and numb that we don't have to look at our unhappiness, but we can't evade it. It's still there.

The way out is to learn some new behaviors that will make you feel good about yourself, whether or not the other person responds. Instead of yelling at your mother, "Good Lord, what are you doing to your hair?" say, "Mom, I like your hair. I'm sorry you don't," because you finally recognize you'll never be able to please her. That's one new behavior.

The next might be asking people for what you need. You can learn that when you want love, instead of pouting, getting mad, or slamming doors, you should try something different. Go to the person and say, "I love you, and I need you to love me back. I'm going to come after you until I get it." In no way is this easy. It takes resolve to make that step toward another human being. But afterward you'll be able to say, "That feels good, being able to ask for what I want, whether I get it or not. At last I'm being honest with myself about my needs." And that's one more new behavior.

Imagine what would happen in the course of reading this book if you could add eleven new behaviors for getting love to your original repertoire of five. Then you'd have a total of sixteen, only four of which are unhealthy. Suppose you learn to take some risks in loving, to reveal who you are. You may discover you can ask for the love you want and give up some of your manipulative behavior. Suddenly, instead of feeling unloved, negative, and down in the dumps 80 percent of the time, you'll feel that way only 25 percent of the time; 75 percent of the time you'll like yourself because you like the way you are dealing with the world.

A mature quality of warmth and intimacy comes from learning to like yourself because you have added behaviors to your personality that you like. These new behaviors are not based upon what other people—including those you love—think loving behavior should be. Instead, they reflect you.

To start this process you must look at the way you grew up, at the way you interacted with your parents, at what was called love in your family. You'll be startled by what you discover about yourself and about them. Think back to the time in your life when you were between the ages of ten and fourteen, during junior high and before high school. Remember where you lived, the house you lived in, the important people in your world.

Choose the person who was significant to you as a mother figure. It may have been a grandparent, a teacher, an older friend or, indeed, your own mother. Ask yourself the following questions, and write the answers down so that you can refer to them at another time.

· Was your mother concerned about her appearance?
· Did she have friends?
· Was she introspective, outgoing, intellectual?
· How did she express her anger toward you? Toward your father?
· Was she capable of expressing praise as well as anger?
· Did she try to run everyone's life by making their decisions?
· Did she smother you by planning your life for you? Did she speak for you without allowing you to speak for yourself?
· Did she depend on others for her happiness? Did you feel responsible for making her feel good?
· Was she genuinely religious or did she teach you to use religion as a way to hide from your own and the world's problems.
· Did she say she loved you?
· Did she reach out and hold or touch you?
· Did she continue her expression of love beyond your childhood years?

The written picture you obtain of the way the two of you interacted will provide some insight for you into the dynamics of your present love relationships. On the surface they may not appear to be the same, but the emotions and feelings that were involved in the former will undoubtedly be a part of your present relationships.

Consider Judy, who had doting parents and a neglectful penny-pinching husband. On the surface, her love relationship with her parents appeared vastly different from the unhappy one with her husband, Dick. But when Judy found the courage to leave Dick, her parents exploded. "How can you do this to us? What will the rest of the family think?" And they immediately canceled the trip to New York they had given her. Just like her husband, they had controlled her through money. He had controlled her by withholding; they had, until the separation, controlled by giving. It took a crisis like this to reveal how Judy had continued with Dick a form of her parents' relationship.

If you want to know how your mate is going to treat you in a long-term relationship, spend a week at that person's home.

Watch how his mother or mother-figure treats him and how he reacts. Let's say your mate is a woman who is sweet and kind to a very controlling mother yet you detect a great deal of underlying anger amid the sugary kindness. Eventually, you will see that anger surface toward you, and then it may not be so well hidden. Then, you must decide either to tolerate the kind of upset you are sure to experience in the future or to discuss these potential problems with your lover, or to look elsewhere for a better relationship.

Few of us are behaviorally creative; that is, our everyday interactions are basically sophisticated repetitions of the childhood relationships we had, something I have already labeled pragmatic love. These modes of behavior are learned from the loving experiences we encountered or observed among our role models.

If you conclude that you do not like the way you related to these loved ones or they with you, then you must choose to learn a new way to love. The magnificence of being human is that you *do* have the opportunity to choose how you will act. Real loving involves making that choice.

CHAPTER 2

Fraudulent Love: Paying the Price

When I was a child, I received an awful lot of love if I didn't put my hands in my pockets. While I watched my father work, he would tell me, "Don't do that," so I would take my hands out and feel assured he loved me. Love stirs up romantic visions of caring and sharing and giving for most people. That's also what all the books say. But I believe that love as we normally experience it may go like this:

It's breakfast time. My wife, whose parents taught her that eating crusts on toast merits love, is at the table eating her toast, crusts and all, and concerned over why she isn't receiving an abundance of attention from me. I am sitting opposite her, my hands out of my pockets, irritated that *she* doesn't notice *me*. She's asking for my love in her way, and I'm asking for her love in my way, but we have failed to get an interpreter. We are all frantically looking for love, but when we go after it, we all follow the same rule: Don't let people get to know you; don't bother to learn their love language; just do the "right thing" and you'll get love. In your house it might have meant wearing a tie and a jacket. In somebody else's house, only unbutton one button, at the neck. The erroneous way we learned to go about satisfying our need for love is one of the fundamental problems all human beings face. My office is overloaded with people doing the "right" thing but having problems with loving and getting along because they have never really come to know one another.

We all need romance, intimacy, closeness, and concern, but few of us ever experience enough of it. Instead we experience anger and resentment; hurt and disappointment; obligation and lack of freedom. That's the reality of love. If you've ever been intimately involved with someone, think of the times when the things you did came not from feelings of "love" but from guilt, or a sense of responsibility, or the fear of being hurt. Those negative motivations are generated by the fear that if we don't do the right thing we may not get that love. And yet we can't always be perfect lovers. Even the best of us fall short at times. We are neglectful of and make life difficult for those for whom we care.

Sometimes love seems like a trap we fall into as if we deserve nothing better. Few of us were ever told that we were worth the price of love. We had to be unusually fortunate to have parents who were able to love us unconditionally, just for being who we were. What most of us got instead was, "Finish your dinner, then you can have your dessert." "Do the chores, then you can go out." Now many of us do the same thing ourselves. Why? Because now we're on the other side. What we're really saying is, "Listen, you are going to go out and be free of us, aren't you? Well, before you leave, assure us that you love us." No one ever said we were O.K. as kids, so as adults when we're late meeting for dinner, we have to explain ourselves: "My goodness, I apologize. My boss needed one last report before I could leave the office. The traffic was terrible! I'm sorry I'm late." But you're not alone, because your friend does the same thing: "I'm sorry! Just as I was running out of the office, Joe called, and I had to sit down and talk to him about one last item. I didn't realize how time had gotten away." For many of us, feeling sorry and having to answer to someone else is just another way of doing the right thing to get love.

It doesn't have to be that way. Years ago, I was sitting at the table with my family. We were eating a beautiful meal of roast with all the trimmings. I had my plate arranged just as I had been taught as a child: meat with the gravy, then the vegetable, then the salad and a piece of bread (probably too much of everything), but it was neat and well balanced. Then I looked over at my son's plate, and it was solid with meat and gravy. I had the terrible feeling inside that something was wrong with the world. I kept looking at his plate and, finally, I said to him, "David, what did you do that for? You only took meat!" "I only like meat," he replied. As a child I would never have dared to give that answer because I was taught that taking just meat wasn't allowed. There were questions he came up with that I never thought of at his age either. When he was about ten years old, he was watching me work when I turned around and said, "Take your hands out of your pockets." Chip off the old block, right? My son turned to me and asked, "Why?" Not an unusual question today, but one which wasn't right to ask your father when I grew up. My own father is now gone and I can't ask him, so I just keep on doing the "right" things. But I'm paying a price to win people's approval: I'm walking through the world scared, scared that I won't be loved. When that happens, my whole world depends on the waiter in the restaurant whom I'll probably overtip, or the policeman I'll politely thank when he gives me a ticket. When I need to be liked, my whole life is dependent on my wife, my kids, my associates, everyone. What a tenuous way to live in the world!

Somehow there's got to be a better way of getting love. There's got to be, because if you love someone, needing them to make you feel sufficient, and they reject you or die, what do you do? Do you beg them to love you and take their abuse, or die with them? It comes down to being so frightened of not being good enough to get love that we must do something to alleviate our fear. What most of us do is avoid the chance of rejection. The cost of doing that is enormous.

Doing the approved thing becomes a way of not letting people get close while making it look as if you were. Now a lot of you are thinking, "Not me. I can be intimate. I let everyone get close to me." I say, "Well, that may be true, but I doubt it. Most of you aren't close to the people you love. You really don't talk very much, and often you don't disclose very much about your personal selves when you do talk. You hide in your everyday existence, even those of you who believe you are getting "close."

A statue in my group therapy room illustrates how relentlessly we create walls between us. It shows two individuals adding a large building block to a thick wall that divides them. The two figures are expending a great deal of energy lifting the block above their heads. So also in life we all are engaged in establishing barriers, and we are willing to expend as much energy to separate ourselves as we do to come together. If this is love, then love is not normal or healthy behavior. Indeed, I believe that real love is so rare that it is not a part of the interactions that most people think of as loving.

We've lost much of our spontaneity, our openness, our

potential for the carefree love that was initially possible for us as children. Even then, the childhood games we played were models for the self-protective kind of love we exhibit as adults. In fact, almost every child in the world still plays a version of one particular game that serves as the prototype for the love games adults play. I have asked individuals from all over the world, and no matter which culture, or color, or language was theirs, the game and the rules have always remained the same. In this country it's called "hide-and-seek," a simple little activity in which children hide from one another. At a signal, one runs after the others, searches them out, catches one child. That child renews the chase, running after the one who tagged him, or anyone else he or she can catch. As adults we run after those who run from us. Sometimes we can reach out and touch each other for a while, just as the children do when touching "home" in the game, but soon it is our turn to run and hide. The child's game seems exciting but harmless; but when adults play at loving, the consequences are far more serious.

We live out the simple childhood game in an earnest emotional game we play: hiding from the persons who could give us the greatest pleasure. Often we run after those who are unavailable.

We like the man or woman who gives us a tough time or who is in love with someone else. And we run away from the person who comes after our love. It accords with the old saying "The grass is always greener on the other side." We keep looking for love elsewhere, but perhaps that searching really doesn't denote indifference or lack of concern or care for what's immediate. Perhaps it demonstrates the difficulty we have in ever allowing ourselves to care for what we've actually got at hand. We are afraid that we might have to acknowledge how badly we need one another. Or we fear obtaining a loving relationship because we don't know if we can sustain the behavior necessary to keep it alive. It's easier to create a nice, safe distance between ourselves and the man or woman we love.

As we mature we learn to hide behind increasingly sophisticated façades, so that "doing the right thing" and trying to please are really very simple attempts at fending off closeness. At first glance, there might seem nothing wrong with doing the right thing—taking care of others, being cooperative, or welcoming gifts. But there is something wrong with devoting your life entirely to others, subordinating yourself to your lover, or needing material displays to prove that you're loved. Sometimes our barriers become a way of life, and they may be very pleasing to other people. A lovely woman may spend her whole lifetime preoccupied with her appearance and what people think of her. She may obscure her feelings of insufficiency by using her preoccupation with her beauty as a protection from getting close. It's difficult to get near a person who is always looking in a mirror. At the same time, were you to ask about her, others would probably describe her as that "gorgeous gal going with Smith. Wow! What a looker!" Not only does her façade protect her from emotional exposure, but it also has encompassed her to the point that no one knows her or suspects her insecurity. Now, there is absolutely nothing wrong with being concerned with your appearance. Instead, it is the degree of concern and the underlying motivation for this concern that I'm speaking about. Walls can be built of any kind of human behavior, be it good or bad, right or wrong, moral or immoral, successful or not. The result of hiding behind the barriers is always the same. The behaviors making up the façade serve both as a screen to obscure our true selves and later as the substance of our character. In effect, we become our façades.

Compulsive individuals spend time making everything

perfect and right, being so concerned and preoccupied with just one specific task that they have no time to get close. Workaholics let work become so much a part of themselves that it becomes tremendously difficult to separate them from the barriers they set up. Funny people present an image of constant humor. They obscure so many other identifying characteristics about themselves that all we see is one big joke. We look at the drunk and see a bottle. We look at the person who's constantly worried about money and see dollar bills.

Sometimes we get so caught up in our goals and aspirations that these too become barriers to the many opportunities for loving available to us. When my wife was pregnant with our first child, I was working at two jobs at night and going to school all day, and she was working as a waitress. There was very little time for us to enjoy her pregnancy, to share the miracle of life. When she was pregnant with our second child, I was away at school in another state, and again we had little time together to reflect on the child moving and growing within her. How many wonderful things go on between us, all of us, every day, that we fail to see because we are so goal-oriented? And in the process, we miss too many of life's marvels.

Professor Spellman was one of my teachers early in my graduate training at the University of Miami. To me, he was a blundering, doddering old man. I thought how unfortunate it was that I had to take his course in Learning Theory 601. Even so, I came into class excited, anxious to learn. I was a go-getter. I already had two or three of my articles published, and I wanted to know everything there was to know about learning theory. What a letdown when this old man sat at his desk and said, "Well, this course is Learning Theory 601. You don't have any books, and you don't have any papers to write. We're just going to learn."

I thought, "My God, there's a wealth of learning theory out there, and this man is telling us there's no text, no papers to write. What kind of geriatric case am I involved with?" I felt so negatively toward him that when the class got together to get him a gift at his retirement, I was the only one in the class who refused to donate. I couldn't, by anything that I believed ethical, donate for a gift to this man, although God knows I was glad to be rid of him.

I came back after Christmas vacation to Learning Theory 602 hoping that I now would have the chance to learn something under a different professor. I walked into the classroom, and Professor Spellman was standing there. The new professor wasn't able to make it that semester. My first question, polite although somewhat facetious, was, "What's *this* course like? What's the difference between 602 and 601?" His answer was, "The number." Then he asked me, "What are you doing this semester, Mr. Reitman?" I pulled myself up in my chair, looked him square in the eyes, and said, "I'm teaching Experimental Psychology 201." He paused, looked at me, and remarked, "That's strange. I teach students." It's twenty-two years since that happened, and if you asked me what I remember from all the courses I took for my Ph.D., it's this remark from a doddering old man. He taught me more than any other professor I ever had. The pain from his remark was so intense that only occasionally do I have to remind myself that I don't see patients, I see people in therapy. I don't have friends, but there are people who are my friends. I don't have a wife, but there is a person to whom I am married.

We are oriented toward rules, objects, goals, anything but people. When we are people-related, we are not always honest even then. We project our problems, our guilts onto them. "It's your fault," we say. "You made me do it."

Then we do not have to look at how we have been the ones avoiding getting close.

We must look at our own barriers, at our own attempts to get love, and not at how others fail to give us what we need.

Waggoner Carr, then attorney general for the state of Texas, once told of attempting to write a speech while his son kept requesting, "Let's play ball, Daddy," despite his repeated explanation that he had a speech to write. The boy persisted, and in desperation Carr decided, "Son, I'll tell you what. I'll play with you, but before I do, I want you to put together a puzzle." With that, he opened the newspaper to an insurance company ad which depicted a half-page map of the world. He cut it up into many little pieces, spread them on the floor, and said, "Go to it!" All the while Carr thought he would have plenty of time to finish his speech. He had barely written the first three lines when his son called, "I'm ready!" The astonished Carr exclaimed, "You can't be! Nobody could put that puzzle together so fast." But his son said, "Oh, I didn't put the world together. I turned the pieces over, and on the other side there was a picture of a man. When you put the man together, the world does O.K. for itself."

If you want to put your world together, it is apparent that you're going to have to put *yourself* together first. You've already looked at how you learned to love from the way important people in your life loved you and each other when you were a child. *Now you must look at what* you *do to get and give love.* Today, if you feel the need for the attention and concern of others, what is the first thing you do? Do you bake a cake, buy a present, take them out, tell them how much you love them? Probably you still do some of the things you did as a child: try to please, cause trouble, get sick, or have accidents. Making a list of those behaviors will help you recognize first, when you are in need of and searching for love; and second, how you go about asking for and getting love. When carried to an extreme, these behaviors may create barriers instead of obtaining the love you want.

Add to the list those personal habits that could be used as easily to separate you from other people as they can to bring you closer. So you might look to see if you are the kind of person who is always feeding people or cleaning up at a party; always reaching for a cigarette or a cup of coffee before you can talk.

Since it is particularly difficult to see yourself clearly, ask a good friend you can trust to share his or her observations of your personality. Do your friends call you the busy person? Perhaps they are reluctant to ask for your attention. Are you the friend who is always cracking jokes? Perhaps you are good for a laugh but not one to be sought out when people need to discuss serious matters. Are you independent? Perhaps no one feels you need them. Do your friends know you as a private person? Most of us will find that we hide much of who we really are behind superficial barriers so that people get little more than a glimmer of the real us.

It also is a good idea to pay attention to the spontaneous reactions of others to us; sometimes they can tell us a great deal about those idiosyncracies we use without thinking and which keep other people at a distance. For example, years ago I was speaking over the phone to our yardman, an East Texas "good ol' boy" with a native country twang. I hung up to find my wife and children laughing at me. When I questioned them I was told that whenever I spoke to any person, my speech took on the inflection of the person I was talking with. I had just done a perfect imitation of the yardman as I was conversing with him. I indignantly denied it, but sometime later I realized what they said was true. If I spoke to an old Jew, I sounded as if I came from the old country; if I talked with Madison Avenue businessmen, I sounded like pure Madison Avenue. I determined then that this was not the way I wanted to get close to others. In fact, this behavior, when misinterpreted, could well offend people.

A list of these characteristics plus your original list describing how you were loved as a child can give you an accurate description of how you now go about loving, yet creating problems for yourself in relationships. Now an examination of why we need these barriers and how we use them in relationships will prepare us for the changes necessary for the experience of real love and intimacy.

CHAPTER 3
Survival Love:
Playing It Safe

Some people approach love like a thirsty zebra on the plains of Africa approaches water. Without water, its life cannot be sustained. However, the zebra is aware as it moves down to the water hole that the lion also frequents this place. Each time the zebra comes to relieve its thirst, the conflict is there: the need for life-giving water and the instinctive recognition that the lion is its natural enemy and that it preys on zebras where they water. As it drifts toward the bank, the zebra does so with great trepidation, ever alert, ears perked, fearfully aware of any sound which may warn it of impending danger. The closer the zebra comes to the water, the more vulnerable it is, for with each step the animal comes nearer the moment when it must lower its head to reach this necessity. Ironically, the moment the animal begins to savor the essence of life, it is more vulnerable to death than at any other time.

So it is for each of us as we approach someone we love. We near the source of our love with fear because we've learned too well that the more we love, the more we care, and the more we can be hurt. How often as children we went to climb up on someone's lap and were told, "No, no, get off! You'll wrinkle my skirt." "No, no! Don't climb up on Uncle John's lap, you'll put your dirty hands all over his shirt." "Now, don't butt in, go play." Of course, children have to learn that there are appropriate times to make their presence known to get the love they so strongly need. But those repeated rejections, so small we usually don't even remember them once we are grown, hurt all the same. In the course of early life, we learned that our proffered love might be ignored, or belittled, or we might obtain a scolding or spanking for our efforts. How like the zebra, who learns quickly that the closer it comes to the thing it needs and desires, the more vulnerable it becomes. How like the zebra, who finds that if it tarries too long around the water hole it may fail to sense impending danger lurking and so lose its life. On the emotional level, we human beings are stamped with the unconscious awareness that the more we give, the more we commit ourselves to loving, the more we risk.

Zebras learn to guard themselves by going to the water hole as a herd. They either hide in the middle of the pack, or on the edge, where they have the best means of retreating, much like people who search for obscurity in a group, or who unconsciously choose a peripheral sense of involvement, thereby claiming membership with only a superficial experience of belonging. In either instance, like zebras, they are involved in protecting themselves. We human beings can no more survive without love than zebras without water. In our own way, we drink from the stream of love warily. Yet how desperately we need it.

Love is so important that even its source is oftentimes irrelevant. Love from a friend, from an acquaintance, love from the shoeshine boy, from the secretary at work, all loving acts directed toward us in the world are essential to our well-being. So very often we become mired in the notion that love has to come from an adored, beloved Mr. Him or Ms. Her to have any value. But that isn't necessarily so. Anyone who has been complimented by the secretary knows that that compliment is as meaningful at that moment as if it came from somebody very important to us—our spouse, or our parents or children. Perhaps it has longer staying power when it comes from someone special, but when somebody spontaneously praises us, it is as refreshing as a cool drink on a dry day.

I recall a story of the positive, beautiful effect that love had on a group of youngsters in a Chicago orphanage. These children were cared for by a group of retarded, adolescent girls from another institution across town. The difference in later adjustment between these youngsters and those who did not share the benefit of the attention given by these special girls was remarkable. The loved children became loving adults. They developed higher levels of intellectual functioning. More of them graduated from high school. They experienced fewer divorces. All this from a little love by individuals with lower I.Q.'s than theirs.

In contrast, there are those who never learn to smile, who go through life bitterly complaining of the inequities it has to offer, who drop out of life and continue to die of loneliness just a little bit more every day. In some instances, it literally is a matter of being loved or dying. I read recently of a four-month-old baby who had died of marasmus, a condition defined in the 1930s. It was discovered then that infants who are not held and touched will waste away. Enlightened as we are, people today are still dying from lack of love, from not being touched and comforted.

Many survivors who suffer from the same emptiness don't die, but instead wither on the inside. In adulthood, the same secretary who brightened our day earlier can destroy us with a word. It doesn't have to be somebody who means a lot to us who can hurt us by saying, "You've been looking bad lately. What's wrong?" It doesn't have to be our lover's comment that we're not performing (when we know it's true), for that remark to have a profound effect on us. Teachers, ministers, friends, youngsters on the playground with us can utter small slights that influence the course of our lives for years thereafter. That's why it's so frightening and threatening to risk being rejected or put down.

One of the most significant statements ever made to me came from a person whose name I never discovered. It was an offhand, critical comment about me that he threw over his shoulder toward someone else. This incident occurred when I was in the service. I was quite young, as yet uneducated, but within the first year of service I was already a corporal in a training facility. I had given an order to a group of older enlistees whom I later discovered were also college graduates. When I ordered, "O.K., fellows, move on—let's get into this auditorium for your class," two of them didn't move. Again I barked the order and one man remarked, thinking he was out of earshot, "Guess we'd better go." And the other one commented, "Ah, why worry about him? He probably doesn't even know who Shakespeare is." And with that they casually sauntered off to the lecture room.

I don't think either of them ever recalled that remark, but it was devastating to me because I did *not* know who Shakespeare was. I immediately went to a book and looked up Shakespeare—which I had a hard time spelling, by the way. I not only discovered who he was, but it also made me realize how much there was to learn. Strange that an offhanded criticism could have had such a positive effect. The hurt from it became the drive that later pushed me toward a Ph.D. I happened to be able to say at that time,

"I'm going to do something about that", but the experience could have emotionally paralyzed me. If criticism can be destructive from people you don't even know, think how damaging statements can be from those whose love you need. No wonder it's necessary to safeguard ourselves from being rejected.

We expend a great deal of effort trying to protect ourselves from the hurts, large and small, of the world or to manipulate those we love to diffuse the griefs that can be inflicted on us. The defenses we use to manipulate people are very similar to the way we handle animals. Think of the cowboy camping out on the frontier and hobbling his horse. Being hobbled enabled the horse to travel a short distance around the camp, nibbling at grass, but left it unable to run away. The cowboy did this (and so do we), partly because he loved the animal, and also because he couldn't afford to lose it. Then there are the vast estates where individuals keep ornamental peacocks, and because they don't want them flying off, crack their wings. Oh, they do it as painlessly as possible. Nevertheless, the birds that strut around beautifully displaying their tail feathers, crowing for the public, are crippled because people need to possess their beauty and so can ill afford to let the birds escape.

Finally, notice how we keep dogs on leashes and behind fences. You walk down the street with your Doberman pulling at his choke collar and you are thinking, "This is *my* dog." However, were you to take the collar off, the dog might bolt, leaving you as fast as possible. How much more sense of ownership might you experience if you were able to walk down the street and say to the dog, "Heel," and he would; be able to say, "Come on," and he would come. But how many of us can take that risk? No, we justify the collar with the fact that, well, there are cars out there, and there are dangers out there, and I'm protecting my dog. And so you are. But where does self-protection end and domination begin? Sometimes it requires more than a collar; it requires a cage to obtain the safest control over an animal. That's why we devise zoos in such a manner that we can get close enough to these exotic objects of attraction. With the growing interest in more humane treatment of animals, we have developed zoos where the animals roam freely over imitation ranges that resemble their natural habitats. The illusion is that you see them in their natural form. Because there are no bars visible, you even have the sense that they are free. But the price you pay for the illusion is the distance you need between yourself and the animal that fascinates you.

Because of our insane loving, we take people we care for and psychologically lock them up to obtain their love. We also choose to do the opposite, to exclude people from our world, or to limit their interaction with us. Think of those you know whom you view as beneath you. You can say, "Well, I don't want to be close to them anyway. They aren't worth it." At once your prejudice shuts them out. But what about the people we want to like us? How do we deal with them? Often, we cripple them. We restrict them by feeding them when they are fat, giving them drinks when they are already drunk. We emphasize their inadequacies when they feel insufficient, all the while taking pride in possessing them and reminding them of their bars constructed of fat, drink, and inadequacy. We may also choose to build our own cages, which serve to surround us but keep others at a safe distance.

If we want an intimate relationship that nevertheless keeps us safe from harm, we merely need to follow Nick's way of thinking. A successful young writer, Nick told me that he's a very sexual guy, yet every woman he's gotten involved with, including his ex-wife, didn't care for sex very much. He concluded that not many women like sex.

"Look at this last girl, for instance." He had spent some time at a border town three hundred miles from home, where he met a thirty-five-year-old woman who had never been married. A devout Catholic, she was still living with her mother and father. Obviously he had to look hard to find this particular person. "But that's the kind of relationship I want," he claimed. When I asked him what he called a relationship like this he replied, "It's an in-depth, distant relationship." The relationships were genuine attempts at achieving closeness; his words more accurately portrayed the emotional turmoil within him, the desire for closeness mixed with the fear of intimacy.

All too frequently we choose to be unaware of our behaviors. They are invisible to us, for these barriers are erected primarily as our defense against the buffets we may endure. We human beings find it very difficult to admit to ourselves that we are frightened. Consequently, we rationalize what we do in our relationships. Rationalization here means that we do not examine our behavior, but excuse ourselves by justifying our actions. We justify how we treat animals and how we deal with people. We justify the fact that we had to do this or that or our child wouldn't go to school. We had to help with the homework because it was so late and it wouldn't have been done. We had to pay the bills because ". . . if I didn't do it, my husband never would and the electricity would be cut off." At the same time, we go through life bitterly complaining of the things we have to do. Rationalization results from our reluctance to look at our real motivations. We fear to take risks, to place ourselves in the hands of others, to be hurt, to be threatened, and to recognize that we must then act in response to that hurt and threat.

Many people who don't want a divorce, who don't want a separation from a boyfriend, a spouse, or parents will accept inordinate pain or a lot of distance in order not to risk losing what they find to be a safe version of love. For example, they explain away the blows they receive from parents because their parents are old, and how can aged parents hurt children at this time in life? They justify a sad relationship by offering an explanation for the other person's behavior, or by hiding the truth of what goes on between themselves and the person they love. June is the kind of person who has never let anybody know what she needs, has never asked. Until recently, she'd never even recognized what had caused her to be upset, because before looking inward she would eat anything in sight. The complacent, ever-jolly June is finally coming in contact with some of the anger she has hidden beneath her fat for so long. Now that she is willing to examine the source of her anger, she is also able to be less guarded and to express what she feels. Barriers are beginning to lift within her life as she confronts some painful truths. She set down on paper some of the realizations she has had. It was not easy for her to confront her grandmother, the one person she had loved most and by whom she had been hurt most.

> Grandma,
> Today you called me. Oh, how nice, I thought! Instead, the anger and hurt that has been inside me for years is beginning to surface. The telephone call was not to see how Ralph or I was or how the weather was in Texas; it was to see if I would let Michael come live with me and maybe in a couple of weeks Granddad could stay with me for a vacation for you. I am not a baby-sitter for you or a nursemaid to a twenty-year-old who is a product of your rearing. Live your life with anything valuable pinned inside the pillowcase you sleep on at night so Mike

won't steal it, but don't expect me to live my life that way or expect my husband to live his life that way, either. How dare you even ask!! And then tell me to do it for you, it would be so much help to you—you want the time alone.

Well, all my life I have been alone. This you well know!!

Thank God I didn't turn out like the boys, but what a price I had to pay for the food, shelter, and clothing you provided. I have come to realize something I guess I have always known and didn't want to admit, and that was that no matter what or how good I did something, there was not going to be anything for June out of it, just a slap on the face about how important the boys are! Stop and think about how I excelled in anything I did! This was for love—love I never got.

Oh, how I hate you for the things you have put me through! But, God, how I wanted your love and attention—anybody's love. Isn't there someone who cares?

No mother, no father, no grandma, no grandad. Maybe June can't even like June; certainly it is apparent no one else does. Oh, except when they want something. Well, want all you care to. June has to find something within herself to start liking, and that doesn't leave room for doing for those who don't care about her.

I'm moved by that letter. It is vindictive and angry, and I wish that Granny had gotten that letter, for June never mailed it. The sadness of it is that old crone wouldn't have been stirred by it anyway. She would think her fat grand-daughter is just being hostile and bitter again and unap-preciative of everything she did for her. For June, just writing the letter was the first opportunity for her to ex-press her feelings. It's the type of letter that opens up a depth of emotion that we don't want to display, even to ourselves.

I believe it is not always the desire for revenge which motivates us to express so graphically what we feel. When we reach out for a taste of love, when we allow ourselves that moment of vulnerability, we are taking a stand, mak-ing a declaration of what we want at the risk of ensuing rejection. Taking that step entails its own set of risks, for we penetrate our own jail of insensitivity and aloneness to experience the grief that comes from recognizing our un-fulfilled need for love. We may even face the painful real-ization that love will never be forthcoming from someone we especially desire. The result can be the moment of truth in which we acknowledge, however briefly, that we are no longer children, but adults who have the power to go out into the world and expand emotionally to include friends, husband, children—in a world in which there is love to be obtained when we have the courage to be vul-nerable. Surviving behind our barriers is not enough. Lov-ing requires the bravest of deeds, the willingness to risk tearing down our walls. It requires turning the key and stepping outside of ourselves to see who we are. Only then can we learn what kind of love we really want from our world.

CHAPTER 4

Status-Quo Love: Fearing to Change

Until now, I've written of the ways people defend themselves from the intrusion of others. Now let's examine the interdependent bonds we form with other people. Most of us, despite our carefully built walls, wind up living with someone, staying at home with parents, or having at least one good friend. In one fashion or another, we develop relationships which sustain us and give us the opportunity to feel that we are involved and that we are truly loving. At the same time, we often establish safe associations that permit us to survive not alone but alone together—relationships that allows us to coexist without exposing too much of ourselves but which nevertheless give the appearance of real involvement. This appearance is not just for the sake of others. Frequently it's used to fool ourselves because we need to feel we're involved and that we love. Therefore we hide behind acceptable screens: work, children, home, community, church activities; for that reason, no one is able to criticize us. The truth is, most of our bonds are formed on the basis of getting along with someone else, not from having developed a relationship with ourselves first, of being comfortable with ourselves. Life's energies seem geared toward one purpose: to establish relationships in which we can live semicomfortably. In them we are willing to lose a part of ourselves to avoid the fear of abandonment or aloneness. We settle—settle for boredom, for uproar, for dissatisfying sex, for peace and quiet.

My dad spent his life settling for giving in to other people. His motto was, "Peace at any price." He extended credit to everybody who came into his small Army-Navy store. People ran up bills and he always had difficulty asking them to pay. He believed most of his debtors to be great friends of his and never admitted that they took advantage of him. He wanted love so badly that he was willing to pay for it.

When you allow that kind of relationship, you take a lot of hell and you have a lot of resentment, but you also get benefits. I can remember my dad's benefit was that he was considered a nice guy. He was truly a fantastically bright, capable man who spoke six languages, but he never believed in himself. All he understood was that you're loved if you work hard, and so he worked, worked, worked. However, he didn't know how to make money sitting down, not "working." He couldn't believe that he could gain wealth with intangibles. An uncle of mine who was very successful in insurance tried to get him to do that. My mother, however, said no, and Dad didn't because he was scared of her. Then once he was going to buy four houses on a little street for five hundred dollars (they had saved up exactly that much), and my mother said, "No, that money is between us and the whole rest of life." Years later, I would hear him talk about how he should have gone in with Uncle Max on the insurance deal or Uncle Lynn with the real estate, or he should have bought those houses. But he didn't do it because of his fear of my mother. By living his life afraid of her, he also bought an insurance policy against ever considering himself a failure because he could always use her as an excuse. In order for Dad really to have loved Mom, he would have had to step out of this relationship and take a risk on his own. He would have had to avoid using his spouse as the excuse to deny his own fear of failure. Instead, he remained caught in a relationship which protected him from himself and from any real loving.

Just like my dad, we settle for situations in which we feel we're getting terribly hurt but which afford us the luxury of not having to look at ourselves. So it is that the person fearful of sex marries someone who turns out to be gay. Years later, she cries about the terrible shock of discovering that she married a homosexual, yet during that period of survival she never had to look at her own fear of sex. A person fearful of intimacy may marry a person who is unapproachable. All the while he is married, he complains about the fact that the other person won't talk, or be involved, or doesn't care. Meanwhile, his own barriers against intimacy are never threatened.

Real relationships should be loving interactions between two independent people, but most relationships serve only as sanctuaries for us, places in which we can hide. In them, we use unconscious, highly sophisticated styles of behavior to guide us safely through a dangerous world so effectively that we are unaware of either the dangers that we face or the means by which we avoid them. I call these survival interactions symbiotic relationships, for they mimic identical relationships found in nature. If we pay attention to their characteristics we can see the same patterns duplicated in human interactions among people whose unhappy ways of loving fit one another.

First of all, this is not a host/parasite relationship, but one in which two creatures support one another's existence. One of the really interesting examples of symbiosis is that of the dentist fish, which swarms around sharks. That seems like an unbelievable thing to do, since sharks eat other fish. Not the dentist fish, though. It swims in and out of the shark's mouth and cleans its teeth while feeding on bits of food collected there. There is a mutual balance between them in which one fish travels with the other, each doing something that's "abnormal." After all, fish don't usually swim into the jaws of sharks, and sharks don't usually allow fish in their mouths unless they intend to devour them. In the case of the shark and the dentist fish, "abnormal" behavior becomes normal for them to develop a means of existence. So also, the termite lives off the wastes of an internal organism that digests the wood the termite consumes. Without the organism, the termite would die from ingesting the wood. In these and all cases of symbiotic relationships, two independent, living beings develop such vital dependence on one another that without the relationship's being just the way it is, neither can survive.

There are many examples of symbiotic relationships in the human world. One of the nursery rhymes we heard as children best parodies it.

> Jack Sprat could eat no fat,
> His wife could eat no lean;
> and so, betwixt them both, you see,
> they licked the platter clean.

How do you recognize when you're caught in a relationship like this one?

1. They are usually long-standing. They keep us going for a long time.

2. They are attachments we find fault with. They are not satisfying, and we openly criticize the relationship and our partner.
3. We voice how we are going to change them, but then we find all these reasons to justify staying on, how we can't change, never will change. We rationalize why the relationship has to stay the way it is.
4. We are totally unaware how necessary these unsatisfying interactions are. The martyr needs the alcoholic mate; the abused wife needs the violent husband; the weak single guy needs a domineering girlfriend; the single gal who feels unworthy needs the kind of man who will dump on her.
5. The reason we need such relationships is so we won't have to change. We put great effort into maintaining the status quo because otherwise we would have to change as well as the other person. Change causes anxiety, and the purpose of symbiotic relationships is to reduce anxiety.

Suppose you have an inkling now that you might be involved in a symbiotic relationship and you *do* want to change it. What do you do now? Well, imagine what would happen if Mrs. Sprat said one day, "You know, Jack, I'd like to eat the lean." You can see that Jack would be shaken. The old "loving" relationship could no longer exist. A new one would have to be formed in which Jack accommodated his wife to maintain their love. Change such as this is frightening. If Jack should refuse, then Mrs. Sprat might opt to keeping on eating fat rather than risk upsetting the relationship. When such a breakdown occurs in an established relationship, one of three resolutions are possible:

1. Neither party changes and the status quo is upheld, but each resents the other for not wanting to change, or for wanting to change.
2. One of the two can leave and dissolve the relationship.
3. The parties reverse roles.

We see role reversal occur when a husband retires and his wife, who has been at home all these years, suddenly finds a job while the husband tends the house. This does not necessarily mean that a couple gets a divorce; many times, even after a divorce, an old relationship is continued under a new set of circumstances. Whether they divorce or not, people will often introduce apparent changes while continuing the old set pattern. A surface role reversal may turn out to be no more than a new way to uphold the status quo. What gives them away is the criticism and resentment they display. One woman used to taking care of inept men is now trying to divorce her latest husband. He's an engineer with a doctorate from a very reputable university, but in three years he has had seven jobs and has been fired from every one of them. When she finally got the courage to say, "I can't depend on you, I can't trust you, I'm going to leave you," he fell apart. "What am I going to do? You are leaving me now when I'm down and out? I don't even have a job. How can you possibly desert me at a time like this?" Now she's complaining about what a weakling he is and how she is trying to help him find a job and get him back on his feet so that she can leave him then. A crazy paradox? Not if taking care of someone else almost totally means love to you. A symbiotic relationship can't persist if anything essential in it changes.

Fortunately, even though we are all caught up in such relationships from time to time, there is a fourth resolution, which permits the development of a strong loving relationship: *If both people are willing to alter their roles, a new relationship evolves based on the interaction of the two emotionally free individuals who choose to love and live together.*

Suppose you've been dating someone for three years. You want to get married, but the other person hasn't brought the subject up. You feel like leaving except that tomorrow he or she may suggest marriage. So you stay against your better judgment and settle for a life-style that isn't what you really want. The result is that you are angry at yourself for giving in, mad at the other person for not marrying you, and afraid that there is nobody else out there for you if you do leave. You can evoke that fourth option. What makes the option challenging and frightening is that it requires taking risks, for you can't be certain whether the other person will agree to the change in status quo. If you decide to go ahead, you must make a statement about what you want to the other person. You could say, "I've put three years into this relationship. I want to be married in two months. I love you and I respect your right to decide not to marry me. I know you may not be able to make a commitment at this time. I'm not trying to force you. I'm trying to set a limit for myself, because if I don't, with each passing day, I'm going to be angrier with both of us. I hope that you will be able to go along with me because I love you very much, but I'm no longer willing to postpone my commitment." What you must do, in other words, is determine what you want, when you want it, and what you will do to get it.

It takes tremendous courage to take this kind of stand in a relationship, so you can understand our need to create and hold on to symbiotic, dependent situations. Perhaps that is why it requires a life-or-death crisis for most people to give up a way of life. For example, if we are faced with lung cancer, we'll then stop smoking. If we have a heart attack, we'll change our eating habits. In relationships, if we catch our lover in an affair, we'll do whatever it takes to keep that person; confronted with losing someone's love, we'll lose weight, agree to counseling, change our whole life-style. Just such a crisis in love may be the only catalyst to force on us the eye-opening awareness of ourselves and the ways we interact. If our life processes work, it's awfully difficult to give them up, but when we see that some effective barrier has collapsed and we're forced to confess that we've got nothing else to lose, then there is a chance we'll decide to change.

Fortunately, it doesn't have to be this way. It is possible to make changes in the way we love and find intimacy before a crisis occurs. We simply have to be willing to take the time to acquire intimacy. Developing truly intimate relationships is an activity that lasts a lifetime. Great changes don't happen overnight. If it took thirty years to create and refine a life-style that you now find is not satisfying, then you cannot expect to change it in thirty days. There is no shortcut for learning how to love. It's a case of three steps forward and two steps back, but it's worth the time, effort, and pain. It also means living with anxiety, because just as the dentist fish perishes without the shark (and vice versa), so it feels as if we are losing part of life itself when we give up our old survival behaviors.

Many times in the course of my work I have watched individuals go through the first steps of realization that relationships they've counted on have to change so they can grow. I've witnessed their acute anxiety because that realization brought them to the point where they knew they would have to alter their behavior—give up, in their overall emotional adjustment, a way of life that had supported them. For some the fear associated with the potential loss of these supports seemed overwhelming. I've heard them cry with genuine emotion, "I'm having a nervous breakdown!" I've tried to tell them that possibly what they were experiencing, though frightening and terrifying, was not an emotional breakdown, but an emotional breakthrough. In this instance, I don't want people to avoid their anxiety and fears. We need these emotions to spur us on. Not all anxiety is destructive.

The blind anxiety at such a crossroads in life is often so great that rather than take a new route, we continue along the same path we've taken throughout our lives. Thus we may recognize that we have such dependent relationships, we may feel that some kind of change is necessary, but our anxiety forces us to stay in a survival relationship. With self-recognition, however, the new anxieties and emotions can force change and make us face new challenges. Sometimes, we deceive ourselves by running away and finding new relationships rather than first dealing with the ones we're in. Such avoidance only curtails positive change and results in the perpetuation of old patterns. First we have to stay and fight.

If you're petrified, run toward what is frightening you, not away from it. That fear means you are getting close to what you badly want. If you can take a stand and stay with it, then in the future you have the opportunity for rewarding emotional growth and satisfaction in genuinely loving relationships.

CHAPTER 5
Controlled Love: Forfeiting Freedom

A good relationship based on real love seems a simple matter. All it requires is that we become free. That means we must divest ourselves of guilt, fear, and reluctance to take emotional risks. That does not mean these old behaviors are completely eliminated. Quite the contrary. The tendencies always remain. Furthermore, we become painfully aware of the taboos we violate when we learn to speak our minds, when we risk having someone dislike us, or, even worse, possibly reject us. In spite of the pain, we come to realize that we are not totally free to love anyone when we fear losing them, or their approval, or their concern. In similar fashion we allow no one to love us in return when we hide from them behind façades built of anger or self-serving compliance. Such methods allow us to control the amount of risk and potential rejection in relationships, but they do not allow others to know us. If to know us is to love us, then the degree to which we are able to give up control and reveal who we are is the degree to which we allow others to love us. Being free means being free to expose ourselves to others and to interact with them openly without deception or manipulation. Unfortunately, being free is rare. *Control is the most common form of love.*

The means by which we establish control are varied and subtle, but the end result is always the same: the structuring of the world into a place in which we are emotionally safe. This structuring process can be divided into two major approaches. The first is the aggressive control of other people's lives and actions. It's easily recognized in the bully, the dictator, the tyrant. These individuals behave in a way that indicates they feel impervious to harm when they can dominate others. Because they are easily recognized, it can be easier to deal with them than with those persons who surreptitiously attempt to control others. Those who use a covert kind of control are manipulative. They subtly control others by making it appear they themselves are the ones being controlled or victimized. Another form of passive control involves basing personal feelings of worth on what you think another person is feeling. These covert methods of control are just as distasteful as aggressive control but are much more difficult to handle emotionally because the weapon they use is guilt.

It is sad to think what our manipulative behavior costs us in the amount of love we give and receive. Margaret has never gotten free of her mother. "I'm fifty-six," Margaret says, "and she's seventy-eight. If I so much as interrupt her unintentionally, she'll tell me to be quiet and insist that I should know better than to interrupt her, so I keep quiet. I have learned never to express an opinion around her. All these years she's never bothered to find out what I think and feel, and I no longer try to tell her." This woman has come to feel a great deal of anger even though she holds her tongue and says nothing. The end result is enormous resentment and restriction of caring. In effect, because she is and always has been unable to risk standing up to her mother, she has never truly been able to love her. Neither her own nor her mother's behavior is at all surprising if we understand that most of us have been taught that expressions of love are both embarrassing and a sign of weakness. For many of us it is almost a sin to admit that we love someone who no longer loves us, or that we love someone more than that person loves us in return. We are intellectually aware that we need to communicate, to demonstrate feelings, and to reach out to our fellow men, but we hide our emotional vulnerability. When we do show our emotions, we often employ one of the several methods of control mentioned above.

When we need to feel victimized, we are capable of taking perfectly safe situations and extracting from them, selectively, the one comment or action that can be construed as hurtful. That is a good way of monitoring the amount of hurt we might endure. Moreover, some of us look for, even cling to the possibility that other people will hurt us, not because we're morbid or masochistic and want to punish ourselves, but because we are insecure. Consequently, we stay on guard, unconsciously, automatically, against all the injuries that may come our way. Give us a gracious compliment and we think, "Uh-huh, I know what was really meant by that. They were putting me down." This behavior is guaranteed to protect us so we can survive emotionally in this world by establishing distance from and control over our encounters.

At the same time, while we are being so careful to avoid harm, we are looking outside ourselves to others to tell us that we are doing all right. It is as though we were to check our temperatures by putting a thermometer in our neighbor's mouth. Most of us go through life determining how we feel by checking the temperature of other people, looking to see how they are feeling about us. Even as kids we did that. If Mommy was unhappy, we hadn't been good. If

Daddy walked in angry, we must have done something wrong, for if we love someone and behave in a certain way, and they happen to become happy or mad, it is because somehow our actions influence their emotions. In effect, we become victims to the omnipotence we felt in our youth. Likewise, in our minds, their reactions determine how we feel about ourselves. The association made then as children between love and control has made the two synonymous in our minds.

Invariably, the first thing we do in so-called loving is to give the other person control over us if we want them to love us. Often our loved ones have no idea of the amount of control we surrender to them, and at the same time, little awareness of the amount of love we are feeling for them. Whether it be hidden or expressed, it is difficult to separate control from love in the adult mind. Fortunately, it can be done.

Ann has a gifted mother-in-law, Helen. Ann has always felt unacceptable and inadequate in Helen's eyes. Even though Ann enjoys her own successes, when she measures herself against Helen, she falls short. Helen recently moved back into town and started a new business. Finally after six months of living in the same town, Ann and her husband (who doesn't feel any better about his mother than Ann does) started to see Helen socially. They were out for dinner one night when the husband was suddenly called to the phone, which left Ann, her mother-in-law, and an associate sitting at the table. The two colleagues were in real estate and very soon were so totally involved in discussing interest rates and mortage plans that Ann felt absolutely left out and unimportant. And yet they were not deliberately ignoring her; she had every opportunity to be part of the conversation. In fact, prior to getting so involved in their talk, Helen's associate had asked Ann what work she did, to which Ann had replied, "Don't laugh, I sell butterfly valves." Her mother-in-law exclaimed, "You know, I just have to block that from my mind! I can't imagine it!" Helen went on to talk exclusively about her own work, leaving Ann feeling estranged. Ann had, at that moment, a terrible sinking feeling, for she realized that her evening had just been ruined. Her mother-in-law had done it to her one more time. "It doesn't matter what I do," Ann felt, "it's not good enough, not even worth mentioning."

Just then, Ann remembered something she had once been told: Say what you have to say. With every bit of strength she had, fearing total rejection, fearing an argument, feeling certain that she was about to be inundated by this strong-willed, single-minded woman, she offered, "I was really hurt by what you said." Taken aback, her mother-in-law asked what she meant. When Ann related how offended she felt at her mother-in-law's comment regarding her work, the woman exclaimed with astonishment, "My God, I didn't mean to hurt you! What I meant was that I just can't conceive how to sell butterfly valves. I don't understand what that kind of valve is to begin with. I can't imagine calling oil industrialists all over the world just to say that I've got butterfly valves I want to sell. I block it from my mind because it just makes my head swim. Ann, I meant what I said as a compliment."

By initially trying to manipulate the situation so that she would not be hurt any further, Ann had totally missed that compliment. How did she exercise control? She withdrew from the conversation. She refused to feel part of the group. She also refused to risk being hurt anymore and did what she could to minimize that possibility by erecting a wall of passive silence. Although she meant to counteract Helen's domineering behavior, her means of handling a potentially painful situation through passiveness and withdrawal were just as effective as overt domination. She controlled precisely how much hurt she would get until that moment when she confessed to her mother-in-law that she had been hurt, until that moment of caring when she left herself wide open to any response—good or bad—from Helen.

The two women spent the next seven hours talking, until two in the morning. During the evening, Ann revealed how bad she had felt over the years that her mother-in-law had never gotten involved with her grandchildren. Helen told Ann honestly, "I never felt I could. Every time I tried, you seemed angry. You seemed to separate the kids from me. You found fault with everything I did. I was keeping them too long or too little. I was instructed on what they could eat and what they couldn't eat. I felt that you didn't want me involved with them unless I did everything exactly the way you would do it. And then they weren't involved with me, they were involved with you, only me doing things your way. If you wanted them involved with a grandmother, then perhaps I had to be able to make my own mistakes and to do my own thing and give them myself."

The story has a happy ending, but the relationship isn't totally resolved. Ann's fear of being controlled and her compensatory manner of controlling will continue, as will her mother-in-law's need to dominate. They will not suddenly surrender those typical methods of protecting themselves. These two women will continue to clash as long as Ann and her mother-in-law choose to love one another. The solution each time will always be the same: taking risks, being honest.

Because loving is an ongoing process, the need to be vulnerable and express oneself is also an ongoing process we must work at throughout our lives. I don't know if there is always a happy ending; sometimes one or both parties may be unable to share themselves at the same time, but there is always another day.

We all possess our own versions of Ann's controlling behavior. Most of us learned subtle lessons in control from our parents. Perhaps the most effective, and at the same time most emotionally damaging kind of controlling behavior is that which elicits guilt. Parental kindnesses were often used as a method of manipulation. "This is being done for you, darling," we were told. "It hurts me more than you, dear." Such parental control is evident on the overt, disciplinary level, but it is present far more on a covert level because most of the control we can permit ourselves as thinking, genuinely caring human beings is passive. This is the kind of control we see so very often demonstrated through denial. It is the kind of control that causes a parent to say, "Sure, darling, if you want to do that, go ahead. You can go even though I'll worry, I'll be left alone, you don't care about me." This kind of behavior allows us to do what we want to do but has a hidden price tag on it.

One of the most prevalent misrepresentations of love is the one in which the child asks a parent for money or a favor. Some of the answers he gets are: "Daddy and I have talked about it, and we said that it was O.K. to send you to this summer camp, but we won't go on vacation this year. You can have the dress, darling, and it's O.K. because I really didn't need the coat I was going to buy. It's almost spring anyway." The tremendous number of innuendos children endure. Or they face the parents, who first argue, but who then succumb overtly, saying, "All right, if that's what you want, go ahead. Go out and do what you want, but if anything happens, it's your responsibility." They are not really giving wholehearted permission, but rather mean, "You can go, you can do as you wish, but don't count on me for support. You're on your own. If you don't do what I want, I'm not here for you." This is a manipulative form of using love and support as blackmail. Love is there when you comply, it is not there when you don't.

Some parents take a whole conversation directed toward some other topic and suddenly turn it into, "Yes, everything's fine and the doctor said I can go off the pills next week." Suddenly it's, "What pills, Mom? What doctor? When did you go?" At once, her children are in the palm of her hand and she never said a word about how much she wanted their love or feels rejected and uncertain of their love. He's the kind of father who mixes his approval with rejection. "She's a great daughter; if only she'd lose a little weight, get married, behave respectably." I am not talking about parents being bad people. I'm talking about all of us and our need to ensure that people care, our need to ensure that they don't hurt us, don't reject us, don't forget us. We're willing to have people remember us in any way we can, by controlling them and keeping them around us; or by forcing them to leave but go out into the world feeling guilty.

None of us can constrain another person's behavior and have the result be a sense of freely loving and being loved. And, of course, when we are threatened in any way, the more it is "normal" for us to institute additional control. The healthy thing is to realize how ineffective our manipulative behavior really is. In fact, we have very little control over other people. There's a story of a kid in the classroom who is jumping up and down, yelling and screaming. The teacher walks in and says, "Johnny, be quiet. Johnny, sit down." Johnny ignores her until she rushes over, grabs him by the hair, pulls him down into the seat, and says, "There now, you are sitting. What do you think about that?" And Johnny replies, "In my head, I'm still standing." We only fool ourselves when we control people's actions. We can't control the inside human being, and when we try to, when we so whip them and take their spirit away, they aren't worth having. Most of us feel uncomfortable exercising that kind of control; that's why we opt for the passive, difficult-to-spot kind of persuasion. And that kind of control is terribly insidious.

I have seen myself do this to my daughter. When Shelly bought her town house, I became concerned for her sake. When I asked about cost per square footage, she wasn't quite sure what I meant. When I asked about the term of the mortgage, she was equally vague. I began an intensive investigation into the price and type of town houses available in Houston, only to find that she had apparently picked the best buy on the market. Then I heard she had told somebody I was upset because she had done something on her own. I denied that at first, but I only had to look at the situation to see that it was true. I was attempting to control her decision, trying to assure myself I hadn't lost my importance in her eyes. Shelly's having the freedom to act on her own makes her a mature individual and gives her the freedom to choose whether she loves me. That liberty is essential for her, frightening for me.

It takes living with a little uncertainty and being able to step back and look at yourself in order to spot when you are being manipulative. There are some easy ways to recognize when you're doing just that. You know you are being controlling when:

- You find yourself wondering what others are thinking about you, and you try to conform to what you think they want.
- You find yourself angry at someone and you don't know why. Chances are you feel victimized.
- You notice yourself avoiding people who might hurt you. (Such avoiding usually brings on additional hurts.)

- You feel you do more for people than they do for you.

It is possible for you to break these patterns of control, even if you've held onto them since childhood. If you have the ability to see what you are doing, you have the power to free yourself. Here are some suggestions for getting started:

- Take chances with people. Share your feelings with them. Caring without control means owning up to the notion that you can be hurt.
- Allow yourself to be free to make mistakes when you love somebody.
- When somebody is angry with you, know that they still can love you, and you love them.

We will never be completely free of controlling behavior, no matter how hard we try. Can you be satisfied with 60 percent of the time? If so, then you should find lots of room for genuine love in your life. You will seldom feel forced by others to do what they want. You will feel less angry too, for giving up control is the beginning of freedom.

CHAPTER 6
Hostile Love: Hurting the One You Love

A thousand-dollar bill falls into your hands. You treasure it, you try to hold onto it. When you finally decide to spend it, someone discovers the bill is counterfeit. Who would have thought?

You and your lover have been enjoying the most wonderful relationship when suddenly she walks out of your life. Or you have been married twenty-five years, built a whole life around your partner. You are shocked when all at once your spouse announces he wants a divorce. These loving relationships were counterfeit and you didn't even know it!

At the very least, you've had moments when, after a particularly close and intimate time, you suddenly feel irritated with your mate. You don't know where the disgruntled feelings are coming from, but they destroy the tender mood and leave you confused about your feelings toward that special person. Your loving doesn't seem so genuine any longer.

How can we tell when love is real and when it is counterfeit? Without a way to determine the difference, we cannot trust our relationships, even when they seem happy. At any moment we may discover that they can prove as false as a counterfeit bill.

The presence of hostility is the chief indicator that some part of our relationship is counterfeit.

Bogus love and hostility go hand in hand. We are generally unaware that the way we love is what generates hostility. Some of us are so "nice," so "moral" that we can't possibly own up to having such hostile feelings, let alone express them toward someone we love. We may swallow our animosity, but its presence, however well hidden, means that there is some element in our relationship that is false.

There are a number of factors that produce hostility, and it's not really so difficult to discover what they are. Love plus obligation, or fear, or dishonesty, or blame equal hostility. The addition of almost any kind of forced or covert behavior to love results in our feeling manipulated and trapped.

Furthermore, hostility is very different from anger. Anger is an immediate reaction to a given situation. Anger, when honestly dealt with, results in resolution of the difficulty and peace of mind. Hostility is a pervasive emotion that gnaws at us and turns up when we least expect it. It never focuses on the real source of our irritation or leads to any solution. Instead, it protects us, providing a smoke screen that hides what we are really feeling. Hostility always crops up when we do not like the way we go about loving and can't admit it.

We should not imagine that people who are never angry are not hostile. It is no tribute to say that your parents had a wonderful marriage because they never argued. If freedom of emotional expression is not permitted, then there is hostility present and a great deal of dishonesty.

The prolonged absence of anger or discord is the second most common indicator of counterfeit love.

Have you ever heard anyone extol the virtues of their parents, "who never had a cross word between them?" Or perhaps, you have heard couples brag, "We never argue." Such statements are intimidating and difficult to deal with. After all, if this couple never argues, never has cause to be angry or raise a voice in a moment of fury, then we that do are clearly inept at love and relationships. Right? Wrong. Total absence of anger is not reflective of a good marriage. The fact is, people who grow up in a home where there is no anger are also growing up in an environment where all emotion, both good and bad, is shunned. The message is: A show of affection, just like a show of anger, indicates weakness. Emotions are phony, artificial, and cause one to lose control.

Linda was reared in such a home. To her, a good relationship meant there was no conflict. The fact that her parents never argued made her think that such a situation was ideal.

Years later, when her own marriage included conflict and discord, she concluded that the relationship was a bad one. Certainly, she surmised, if there was conflict, it automatically meant there could be no love. What she didn't understand was that arguments can mean something as simple as the presence of two people who don't quite understand each other. She didn't realize that conflict between a couple can also convey the healthy signal "Hey, we've got to do something about this."

Linda had to learn that her husband's volatile nature was actually his own way of attempting to communicate, to state his position. The intensity he used in communicating his feelings stemmed from his fear of being controlled, of being considered less than a man. The booming volume of his voice in no way pronounced "I don't love you." Rather, it reflected the degree of insecurity he felt.

Does this mean that all explosive behavior is reflective of love? Of course not. It does mean, however, that we must learn to distinguish between the two and keep anger and love in their proper perspectives.

Fear also produces counterfeit loving. So many times in a gathering of people, I've watched a person talk while secretly looking at his partner to read her expression and to calculate her reaction. Her response determined whether he felt adequate. I could almost hear him thinking, "Did I offend her? What is she going to think? I've got to go home with her after this; what am I going to face when I climb into bed tonight?"

We must understand that such "love" is not genuine, that even as we look toward the other person to measure how lovable we are, we begin to resent the person. And the indignation grows. We can often be blind to this resentment, unaware of its presence. Inside ourselves, we build up a reservoir of bitterness that stems from our fear of losing love we can't live without. We are upset with ourselves, but we are not aware of that, so we direct our animosity toward those we care the most for.

That's why we observe so much rage in men, rage that can be triggered at the snap of a finger. If Joe feels he has to do all the things he doesn't want to keep Sue's love, then when she tells him she loves him, it only heightens his feelings of being stifled by the fear of losing her. He may offer the appropriate polite response, but inside him that gratitude sparks resentment that may find outlet later in an angry outburst over a trivial matter.

Women experience a similar rage, most evident where sex is concerned. After intercourse, when the man tells her he loves her so much, the woman may not quite believe what he says. From her heart she likes to be told she is loved. But from the pit of her stomach rises an indefinable resentment that translates to, "You S.O.B. When we don't have sex, you don't tell me you love me." She may never verbalize that, but she may forget his clothes at the cleaners, burn the dinner, and have headaches.

When men and women harbor such animosity they may have good reason, but the majority of the time their resentment stems from doubting they can keep love without focusing on the other person's needs and desires. As a result, they are so intent on watching the other person that they fail to enjoy the love that really could be there for them.

If Joannie feels incomplete without a man in her life, then she will go to enormous lengths to keep one around. Her need is so great she loses her spontaneity, her sense of humor, her independence. All is obscured behind a veil of anxiety and resentment as she looks for the meaning behind her partner's every action.

When you doubt you are worth loving, when you feel you cannot be enough for other people, when you are afraid to lose them, you will do anything to keep them. You will deceive them, like the man who lies about his past, or try to perform like the woman who must constantly try to be sexy enough. Or perhaps you just do your boyfriend's wash or fix your girlfriend's car over and over, when it is the last thing in the world you want to do.

So long as people are afraid of losing love—any love— in their intimate relationships, their efforts at loving will result only in discord and self-defeat.

That is not what we were taught, however. We learned that love is being unselfish, giving without expecting anything in return, certainly never asking. That's why many people think that loving a child is the one time they can drop the double messages sent by love and hostility and just be themselves. But small children and babies don't give a great deal. Most of us want more than any child could possibly give.

The most beautiful expression of love is reciprocal love. I need that kind of love. I need somebody who is going to be able to take care of me, too. No child can take care of me. I need somebody who can understand me, and no child can do that.

If what I just said sounds selfish, I intended that it should. Perhaps the most genuine form of loving is selfishness. *In real love we exercise the right to ask for and expect love back from other persons we care about.*

I don't mean that we expect love 100 percent of the time. Obviously there are occasions when we must be first to extend ourselves, when it is our turn to reciprocate or offer love to a mate or a friend. In times of trouble or sickness, concern or weariness, in moments of great or small importance, we must do the giving and caring.

Nevertheless, we ought to be selfish enough to ask, if somebody never gives us very much, why we owe them love. Are we supposed to love them because they are our mother, our sister, our son, our husband? We do not have to love anyone who does not return what we give them. As a consequence of knowing that, we are free to love better than ever in our whole lives. We can love with less dependence, less desperation. And we can expect love back, though perhaps not that minute, that day. Sooner or later, however, we can tally up our giving and taking, and if what we get doesn't pretty much correspond with what we have given, then we can look for another person who does want to give back to us.

We do not have to justify our right to be loved. We needn't feel obligated to perform or to prostitute ourselves. Genuine love is available to us, and it has nothing to do with our sex, income, or beauty. It has to do with a sense of self-worth. When we know we are worth loving, then all the hostility can be discarded.

Obtaining genuine love begins with a rational self-interest which requires that we do what we want for ourselves in our relationships.

I am not excusing self-indulgence. I am suggesting that genuine love requires taking care of ourselves in the long run. When you do for yourself, you can do for others. It's the person who is able to say no who can say yes without spite. When you start to do things for yourself, you like yourself better, and while you may get angry, you're not hostile. How does this work?

Let's say I have agreed to go to a party with you. I am going because I feel I have to. I am obligated to do so to buy your love or to avoid an argument. When I go for one of these reasons, I guarantee you I'll put out enough energy to spoil the evening even for myself. I hope things *are* bad!

If we go to a restaurant I don't like, I secretly hope the food is inedible. I want to complain about the musicians if we're at a dance. I find fault with the company if they're your friends or relatives. I'm going to find something to be upset about.

Now, when I go because I have decided that I want to be with you, that it pleases me, then I'm not about to spoil your fun or mine. When my love is counterfeit, I'll tell you, "You want me to go, I'll go. But I won't like it." When my love is real, I can say, "I'm not really interested in this party. You want to go, and it means something to you to have me there, too. I want to be with you. I'll go. And I'll enjoy myself."

Sometimes we avoid such decision-making because suddenly, whatever we do, we take responsibility for it. I'm here at this party and if I'm unhappy it's my fault, not someone else's who made me come. All at once I'm owning up to everything I do, but at the same time, I have the right to ask for what I want and need.

Doing as we please doesn't mean we'll never give in to

anyone again. Sometimes we make concessions, but that doesn't mean our love is counterfeit. We all bend at times because we need other people. If Jim and Elaine are invited to the lake home of a trusted friend at a time when they would both prefer to stay home, if they make the decision that it's worth the friendship to go, then they forfeit the right to complain. They can make the best of it and even enjoy it.

It can be a terribly uncomfortable lesson to learn to be responsible for yourself. No longer can you complain about the other person. You can't blame them for what happens to you, as well.

For instance, Stuart was a city guy who wanted farmland very badly. His fiancée didn't say that he shouldn't buy it, but she made it clear she would hate living on a farm. Stuart was scared to make the purchase anyway, because it would have meant risking every cent he had. After much consideration, he didn't buy it.

Two or three years after their marriage, oil was discovered on that same land, and Stuart heard himself complaining, "Do you know why I didn't buy that land? Because you didn't let me." His perceptive wife replied, "You didn't buy it because you didn't have the guts to. If you had wanted to buy it, you would have."

Stuart was too hurt at the time to say so, but later he admitted his wife was right. He could not blame her for his decision, however much he wanted to. It would have been a good time to become hostile, to vent his resentment at his wife's inability to admit her fault in the matter. In fact, until Stuart took responsibility for his decision, he could have felt trapped by his marriage to a straightforward woman. Accepting accountability for his decision not to buy melted away any hostility toward her.

Like Stuart, you can be sure you will experience some hostile moments in your life. That hostility need not undermine and destroy your relationships. When you feel those undercurrents of resentment, ask yourself what you want, and then make the decision to do what will satisfy you most. Finally, you have the opportunity to accept the consequences without complaint or blame.

Unlike thousand-dollar bills, love comes our way in abundance. Capturing it for ourselves requires acting on an uncomplicated formula: Loving feelings without feelings of obligation, dishonesty, or fear of losing love is real love. Stated positively, loving feelings added to honesty about our desires and needs lead to a wealth of genuine love.

CHAPTER 7

Sexual Love: Forced to Respond

Years ago some young, and naïve but adventure-some men of the times caught a disease called gold fever. They ran off to the mountains, the hills, the creekbeds, and they searched for fortune. Many of them, because of their inexperience, found veins of fool's gold and, thinking they had struck it rich, registered their claims, dreaming of untold wealth and riches, only to have their bubble burst.

Similarly, many men and women today get caught up in what I call "fool's love"—sex—only to discover that the claims they staked and the romance and happiness they dreamed of were short-lived. The problem: They were naïve, inexperienced in real loving, and unable to differentiate between the real thing and the counterfeit. Love is more than sex.

Real love is the blending of one's emotions and thoughts with those of another person, whether or not sex is involved. It is courageous, without guilt, and without anger.

Nevertheless, no discussion of love would be complete without reference to sex and the complex manner in which the two behaviors are related. Inability on the part of many individuals to distinguish between sex and love causes inevitable confusion and emotional problems in relationships. Sex and love are not the same, yet we often refer to them both as love.

It is common for people to say that they made love the previous night when what they mean is they had sexual intercourse. They may or may not have experienced love. You can have intercourse with love; you can have intercourse without love. Similarly, we can love one another with sex or love one another without sex.

Thus, people frequently hear me insist, "No, you did not necessarily make love last night. You had intercourse. If during, before, or after the experience you shared real love, you added another dimension to the act. But just having sex isn't love." We may understand this intellectually, but if we do not accept it emotionally, we will misinterpret and confuse the two. In our society, if you are a woman, you may offer sex thinking you'll get love in return. If you are a man, you may promise love to get sex.

Still, sex is promoted in movies, books, and television as the most beautiful example of loving, the ultimate illustration of closeness and warmth. They fail, however, to tell the whole story, that sex is a basic physiological drive, always has been, always will be. No more, no less. It is a need within all of us that takes on as many meanings as we ascribe to it. It can reflect a multitude of attitudes. How sex is used or abused depends on the individuals involved.

We like to believe that we live in an enlightened age, that we are more at home with our sexuality and that we feel better about our bodies than people of an earlier era. We are more liberal and more open in our expressions of physical love. We are fascinated with anything that will teach us more about our sexuality. However, books that propose to show women how to make love to a man may only demonstrate to them new techniques for sex. They will not enable them to achieve real love. And a romance begun at a resort does not guarantee a man that he knows how to find love any more than erotic films or novels do.

Marriage doesn't end the confusion between love and sex. Even though both men and women may regard it as the solution, marriage provides only a different setting for acting out the same problem.

When I first met Steve and Angela, they both agreed that sex was the chief issue in their marriage. Was it exciting, satisfying, frequent enough? "None of those," they agreed. Said Steve, "It's not exciting when I always have to beg for it. It's not satisfying when Angela is so indifferent to sex. It certainly isn't frequent enough." Angela's response: "I don't see why it has to be such a big deal. If Steve weren't so demanding we might both enjoy sex more."

When the two got to talking to each other about what they really wanted, the problem wasn't at all about sex. Angela wanted to be wined and dined even though they'd been married for some years. "I never feel special anymore," she complained. "I want some time without the children for just the two of us." Angela longed for moments when Steve would talk to her and share his deepest feelings with her, moments when he would simply hold her.

If Steve had never been content to do just that for Angela, it was because for him sex meant being important to a woman, meant she loved him. Her refusal, or having mechanical sex, said, "She's totally turned off by me, she doesn't care. I don't matter; she doesn't love me any longer." No wonder he reports feeling hollow and empty so often in his life, while Angela herself frequently avoids intercourse. Once again the battleground is sex, but the war is over intimacy and loving.

For many men, love is sex; for many women, love is not sex.

Unfortunately, as liberated, sophisticated, and knowledgeable as we pretend to be, this basic concept represents the rule rather than the exception in our relationships today.

The double standard, though openly criticized, is still the rule, also. Men continue to be indoctrinated with the notion that sexual intercourse correlates with their masculine adequacy and suggests strength and manliness. When they get into bed, women generally want a man with experience, with proficiency, someone who can instruct his partner. Inexperience and awkwardness are still seen as weaknesses rather than as tributes to a man's celibacy or his respect for women.

Sex still represents conquest. A man feels that when a woman agrees to intercourse, she has given in. He has won a contest of sorts. It also means that she must genuinely care about him. It's reasonable that if such a man needs reassurance that he is loved, he will seek this reassurance through sexual consent.

Women want to know that they are loved also; but society still conditions them to see love as not sex, even though they are now allowed a double standard of their own. Women know all about men who want nothing more than to take them to bed, have sex with them, and leave them for someone else. "All they're after is sex" remains a common phrase, and most of us immediately know who "they" refers to.

As a result, when a man says, "Let's make love," there is little doubt in the mind of most women what he means. A woman's early script was, "Before I can give myself to you, I have to know you love me." It has been replaced by the newer one, "You turn me on, I'd like to have sex with you," but the orientation has not changed. Women may know otherwise intellectually, but emotionally speaking, sex without love means being used.

Typically, men have been taught something different, that emotional demonstrativeness implies a lack of masculinity, with three exceptions: anger, aggressiveness, and sexual desire. He certainly isn't supposed to cry, to be frightened or weak, to feel empty and hollow inside like Steve. He is permitted a sense of guilt and obligation to women, and while women are taught to manipulate them into marriage, men fear being trapped in a situation they can't leave with honesty or graciousness.

Nor, for that matter, are men supposed to feel sentimental except perhaps prior to or during sexual intercourse. Then a man can let his guard down briefly. After all, wasn't he able to get the woman to respond, hadn't he met the challenge and conquered her? At that moment, he is safe from being looked on as the vulnerable partner.

Therein lies the key to understanding the difference between the way men and women approach loving. Vulnerability differs between men and women. *For a man, the open expression of emotions represents vulnerability. For most women, sexual intercourse is the ultimate form of vulnerability.*

Without any doubt, it is difficult to stand emotionally defenseless before the opposite sex. If loving and being vulnerable are the same, then a man is going to approach the tender state of love with caution. He's very likely going to look for sex first as in Steve's case. Similarly, a woman is going to approach sex by wanting to be respected, to be held next to a man's heart first.

So when a woman says, "Show me that you love me," what she really is saying is, "Pay attention to me. Lie next to me and hold me. Show me that you want more of me than just my body, that you're not just wanting sex. Be close to me, share your thoughts with me." It is especially important that a man reveal what he is feeling, perhaps because women place much more value on feelings and thus understand the nature of love better than men do.

When it comes to the emotional manifestation of love, women express themselves more easily. From childhood they are generally given permission to be demonstrative. It's all right for women to cry, to give vent to the sensations that well up inside them. Even so, they continue to believe that if they have wonderful feelings toward one man who's willing to marry them, they must be in love and it's acceptable to have sexual intercourse with that man.

Whether a woman is fourteen or forty, without infatuation and a hint of commitment, sex is not quite nice or good. Without these prerequisites, sex for a woman involves the risk of being hurt or used by men. The main way to counter being used remains the same: Contrive to get the man to propose marriage or at least promise to stay together always.

You would think that current morality would have changed these old concepts entirely, but it hasn't. For men and women alike, modern sexual attitudes have done little else than alter sexual behavior in the direction of increased promiscuity. When you get down to basic truth, more people are doing it than can talk about it or understand the real connection between love and sex.

The inner attitudes, the ones that control our feelings and emotions, the ones we unconsciously but very effectively transmit to our children, are still those of the past. Much of the turmoil and conflict revolving around the issue of sex and love result from individuals finding themselves behaving in a new style while thinking and feeling according to old notions. The breakdown between new behavior and old feelings spells trouble for men and women.

Today people are trying to understand and obtain love

through new, permissive forms of sexual behavior. One consequence of greater sexual license on the part of women as well as men is the devaluation of sex. When it is easily obtained, the edge is taken off the excitement and mystery that surrounds it. The consequence is that we are beginning to suspect that love and sex are not the same, and the greater burden is no longer on sexual perform-ance but on loving.

The real revolution is not sexual, but a revolution in learning how to love.

The positive value of the sexual revolution is that it is contributing to widening the gap between associating sex and love. It is becoming easier to see that sex alone is coun-terfeit love. In fact, when we love better emotionally, we naturally function better sexually. What we need is not so much a handbook for better sexual techniques, but a set of instructions that will make available to us the love we want, a set of instructions that both men and women can use effectively.

Our new guide should begin with the recognition that love and sex mean different things to men and women, and therefore the rules for men and women vary slightly.

Men must express their feelings of love. Women must express their sexual desires. Both must be willing to talk more openly about their own unique and individual wishes for love and for sex.

Men must ask themselves what they want in terms of commitment from a relationship. Women must know what they are willing to give physically. Both must keep before them what they want as the physical and emotional out-come of each relationship.

To that end, men have to realize that having sex and experiencing loving feelings at the same time don't trap them in a relationship. They do *not* have to marry the person, to become responsible for her well-being, to promise what they do not wish. Ironically, being free of this trap releases them to express their feelings more freely.

If women are now free to engage in sex without marriage, they are also free to ask to be held, to ask for demonstrations of affection without going to bed. If a woman does go to bed with a man, it can be simply the expression of her physical needs without obligating her to fall in love and commit herself to that man. Women need not make every sexual encounter the romance of a lifetime. Instead they can have sex, be infatuated, and still not be in love, as they choose.

If it is true that men feel more free to engage in sexual behavior and women more readily have entrée to their own feelings, then they have a great deal to learn from one another.

With the aid of women, men may discover that the open expression of feelings need not be indicative of weakness or be accompanied by sex. Women may learn from men that they have permission to experience and express their own sexual needs without the fear of being used or the need to delude themselves and their partners into thinking that their sexual behavior is a testimony to some permanent commitment. Only then can we learn to distinguish between "fool's love" and genuine involvement. Only then can we come to know that there is no more meaningful experience than having the freedom to blend our inner feelings of warmth, caring, and vulnerability with the honest expression of our sexual desires under a protective umbrella of love.

PART II
Real Loving Is Possible

CHAPTER 8

Decisive Love: Going After What You Want

L ove is blind. You've heard this all your life. But does it really have to be?

No. Yet the opposite often seems true.

We think we've made sure that this relationship is different, so much better than the last one. Then the days, the weeks, and the months pass, and here we are again, back in the same situation we left. We're hurt. We're sad. And we're really confused. How did this person change so much since we first met? The softness, the strength, the intimacy, and the wonderful sex we initially experienced are now dim in the memory, and all we can think of is getting out. But to what? And to whom? And even if we do leave now, will it be any different next time?

Perhaps, but so often it isn't, and all our relationships will eventually prove disappointing if we approach love with the definitions found in storybooks, romantic novels, and the uncertain concepts Mom and Dad conveyed to us through the years.

Fairy-tale expectations will get you nowhere in love.

They fool you into believing that love is easy, painless, and that you can live happily ever after. It's like teenagers at an amusement park. They race about skipping, dancing, holding their arms around each other, riding the rides, and finally ending up in the tunnel of love. But life is not an amusement park, and love is not a carnival ride complete with balloons and cotton candy. In the real world of love, you don't get on any of the rides unless you pay the price.

But what is that price?

A willingness to be open and vulnerable, to take a chance on being hurt.

John is an engineer I see regularly in my practice. His life revolves around three things: his work, his home, and his garden. He has few problems with people because he tends to insulate himself from them. When relations involve too much emotion, stress, or conflict, he controls the hurt and pain by refusing to become involved.

When his son, Greg, flunked out of engineering school, John responded by working harder and longer hours, by reading more professional journals, and by taking on more involved gardening projects.

John should have been devastated by Greg's failure. His child was in deep academic and personal trouble. This was a time for genuine concern, yet John managed to weather the storm with little emotional effort.

He was even oblivious to the stress his wife was experiencing. He barely noticed her depression, the number of late hours she spent watching television and sleeping in the middle of the day. He didn't smell the objectionably stale odor permeating every room, where abundantly overflowing ashtrays gave proof to the second pack of cigarettes she was smoking each day.

Imagine his surprise when, during a turbulent and bitter tirade one evening, she announced that she was leaving, that she was tired of living with a robot. What she and her son needed, she screamed at her astonished husband, was attention and love.

"A paycheck and a man around the house," she stated flatly, "won't cut it with me any longer." His wife had had it with a man whose feelings were so dulled that he was unable to get upset enough to care about the people he was supposed to love the most.

Love doesn't come freely and easily. John lost his wife and son because he wasn't willing to pay the price of love, to become involved, to hurt when there was pain, and to let the ones he cared for inside him.

THE "SAFE LOVE" TRAP

The word "safe" has a comforting significance to most of us, but "safe love" is destructive love. It is the great pretender of emotional involvement. If you have ever given your wife or girlfriend an expensive piece of jewelry hoping such a generous gesture would somehow convey, without your really having to say anything, how very much she means to you, then you have been guilty of "safe loving."

If you've ever been embarrassed to admit you were jealous of the cute blonde at the cocktail party who was radiantly fascinated by your husband's witty talk, then you have been guilty of "safe loving."

How many times have you had warm, loving thoughts that you failed to express verbally? They may have ranged from "Your hair looks really nice" to "I thought of you while driving home, and I drove a little faster." Later you may have realized, ever so briefly, that you hadn't told him or her, but if you quickly excused yourself with a thought such as "They know I love them," then you've been guilty of "safe loving."

Unfortunately, there are times when our inability or reluctance to verbalize has far greater consequences than the loss of a golden opportunity to strengthen a loving relationship. All of us can recall times when we were called upon to comfort a friend after a tragedy or the death of a loved one. It's never a comfortable time. It's a duty, an obligation no one enjoys, yet if you are a good and decent person you will be there to help a friend through a difficult time.

But what are you supposed to say at delicate times like these?

I'll tell you what most people say. They say everything but what they ought to say. If you listen closely, you might hear a quickly fleeting, "I'm so sorry about Joe. You know how much we all loved him." After that, it's "Can I bring a meal over tonight?" or "Are there any phone calls I can make for you?" or worse yet, they ignore their grieving friend altogether and begin making busy, commiserative conversation with all the other folks who came by to "comfort" this friend.

No wonder many people admit to having a strange, empty feeling of alienation and rejection after a death in the family. Everyone was there. Everyone helped out. But the death itself was ignored. At times like these, our feelings of fear and helplessness are so overwhelming, we avoid saying the very things that are most important. A friend who loves honestly takes the time to get to the heart of the matter.

"I know there are no words I can say that make you feel better, that make Joe's loss any easier to bear. When I see how you're suffering, I say to myself, 'There but for the grace of God go I.' I want you to know that I'm here and I love you."

The feelings are there in all of us, but often the willingness to express them is not. When you allow these feelings to come out, when you express them, you are putting "safe love" to rest.

THE SIX REQUIREMENTS OF LOVE

If "safe love" is wrong, then how can you recognize and experience real, honest love? What are the requirements for loving the right way?

Learn to talk, touch, and reach out. We cannot wait for others to love us first if we are to have any love for ourselves. We have to ask for love, realizing all the while that sometimes we won't get what we ask for. It's hard to do, but we must force ourselves.

Jack told me this story about the first time he asked for love.

It was a terrible time for him, and for a good reason. Jack had failed miserably on a project that could have meant untold dollars to his company. His boss was mad, and it was clear that any promise of a promotion for Jack was no longer a reality.

In the midst of his depression, Jack's girlfriend called. She was happy and excited. Her day had gone well, and she was looking forward to the weekend. After a while, he found he couldn't bear her cheerfulness any longer. Here she was laughing and joking, and he felt horrible. It was infuriating. He was getting madder and madder at her for being happy. He almost lashed out at her, but he caught himself. Instead of lashing out, he reached out.

"I'm devastated," he found himself saying. Quietly and unashamedly he admitted: "I know you're feeling good, but right now I feel terrible. Right now, I need you to listen to me and to love me."

Reach for love. You may never get it if you don't go after it.

Learn to accept your fears. Running through all of us is the awesome fear that other people will find out what we really are. We are embarrassed that we aren't "good enough," that we don't "measure up."

Recently I was invited to a party at one of our local universities. At one point I found myself standing between two absorbed English professors. They were discussing literature, and I was lost. They mentioned books I'd never heard of and some others I'd almost forgotten. I felt dumb. I couldn't compete. I was not in control. So what did I do and how did I react?

I found myself trying to change the subject. If I could get these two fellows involved in a discussion about photography or fishing or better yet, psychology, they would never find out how very little I knew about literature. Then I would feel good about myself again.

Only when you begin to accept yourself as a mortal human being who cannot know everything or be everything can you really begin to love yourself and others. Only when you can accept the fact that you are allowed to feel inadequate, that is it acceptable not to be in control all the time, can you really open yourself up honestly to others.

Learn to laugh at yourself. So often we take ourselves too seriously. If we laughed at ourselves, the other people in our lives might take it as a sign of weakness. They might think we were foolish or imperfect.

My children never love me as much as they do when I flub and make the same mistakes I've corrected them for time and again. Once, when they were small, I remember giving a mighty dinnertime lecture on the evils of spilling milk. In the middle of making a point about carelessness and wastefulness, my wildly gesticulating arm knocked over my own milk glass. You can imagine the uproarious laughter that followed. But none of it was mine.

I was angry, and the words "You made me do it" begged to leave my lips. But just as I began blurting them out, I recognized the absurdity of it all. I looked foolish and I knew it. I too began to laugh, and as a result, a loving situation opened up for all of us.

When we start to feel good about ourselves, when we begin to understand that it isn't necessary to be perfect, then we can afford some humor at our own expense.

Read between the lines of other people's behavior. Listen with a third ear to the people around you. If you look beneath the surface, you can bring more sensitivity and understanding to your relationships.

A young woman's boyfriend stood her up. She was upset. She was hurt and humiliated. So who did she get mad at? Her roommate.

She told her friend what a slob she was, how she could barely stand to share the same apartment with her, and how she had best shape up.

How is that poor, messy roommate supposed to feel about this? Not good, I'm sure, but if she bothers to look further into her friend's emotional state, she can better come to terms with this outburst.

We can spare ourselves needless anger and hurt if we realize that those closest to us often make stinging statements, not out of maliciousness, but out of their own sense of inadequacy.

Be willing to tell other people what you don't like about them. Without honesty, there can be no love. If an important person in our life is doing something that upsets us, then we should be willing to speak up and say what's on our mind.

This can mean embarrassing admissions such as, "Your

breath smells bad," or "You have body odor." It can mean telling your boyfriend you are hurt every time he says he'll call and then doesn't. It can also mean telling your wife you think she is too hard on the children, that she should try to show more understanding.

Martha hated her husband's annual Christmas holiday fishing trip, but she steadfastly refused to say anything. She felt that a good wife would be nice enough to keep her mouth shut and let her husband enjoy his vacation. But what was happening while Martha was being a "good wife"? She was resenting her husband and wishing him every miserable moment on his trip. By being dishonest, she was hurting her marriage.

Love is not always niceness, sweetness, or goodness. Often real love involves harsh realities that aren't easy to face but are nevertheless testimony to the courage and honesty of someone who loves enough to speak the truth.

Commit to change. There are things you don't like about yourself. Maybe you're too fat, or you smoke, or you are guilty of exploding into nasty temper tantrums. Maybe you can't say no and you allow others to run over you, or maybe you are a perfectionist who expects more than other people can possibly give.

You have seen your faults. You know what they are. Still, that isn't enough. You must begin now to change these things that bring you unhappiness and stand in the way of your loving and being loved. Don't give up on your problems by falling back on the old excuses: "You know that's the way I am," or "You can't teach an old dog new tricks."

If you are trying to improve yourself, then these can no longer count as valid excuses. A whole new world opens up to those who change the way they react to the problem areas of their lives.

WILL THE "RIGHT PERSON" BRING HONEST LOVE?

It is easy to blame the other person for all the problems of an ailing relationship, but we must be cautious in our search for the "right person."

Of course, we don't love just anybody. Some spark is necessary, some kind of chemistry has to exist. But there are far more than one or two people in this world with whom that chemistry can develop.

In some ways loving is like keeping a fire alive. First there is a spark of flame, that initial bloom of interest, that certain something that catches our eye and says, "This is a very special person." But once that spark is there, it requires effort to keep it going, or it will surely die. You must trouble yourself to cup your hands around the spark and help that fire to burn.

This is the same kind of care and effort most people exert when they first begin to date. In the beginning, they guard the relationship carefully. Doors are opened, words are carefully chosen, birthdays are remembered and so are anniversaries and special holidays. There are favorite little restaurants and warm, sentimental songs. Both people are going out of their way for the other, not necessarily because it's right or proper or good or moral, but because they want that person to love them. Consciously and calculatingly, they are attempting to make all their behaviors, all their actions say: "I am a loving person and I want to be loved. I want to give love, and there are many things I am willing to do to get it back."

Such affections are meaningful and important, but I think we give far more value to these kinds of romantic expressions than we should. Do not misunderstand. They are part of showing your love, but by no means all of it. Everyone revels in the exultation and attention that go with sentimental love gestures, but over the long haul, on a day-to-day basis, the honest loving that takes place as a result of conscious thought and decision is the kind of love that wears the longest.

Honest loving requires inner effort. It requires more than bothering to show up on time for a date, or remembering to return a phone call, or trying to look your sharpest and sexiest for an evening out. Honest love does not mean buying something or making someone the center of your life, nor does it always mean being nice.

The man who can say to his woman, "I know you think I'm big and strong; I know I lead you to believe that nothing scares me, that I can handle anything, but I want you to know that sometimes I'm frightened and sometimes I'm scared" is a man who is offering real, honest love.

The woman who can say to her man, "I know that I've told you that marriage doesn't interest me, that all I'm out for is a good time, but I haven't been telling you the truth because I was afraid I would scare you away," is loving honestly.

Real, honest love involves risk, but if we're not willing to risk losing love, we may never gain any.

CHAPTER 9

Honest Love: Giving Open Love

Do you remember your first date as a teenager? How scared, awkward, and clumsy you felt. Recall how much trouble you took to dress and how concerned you were about knowing what to say all night. And do you remember how you were teased about your concern? You were probably told, "Grow up, kid. Act your age!"

It's no surprise that people cover up their tender emotions with anger and indifference or that they experience sadness, aloneness, and upset while trying to find love. But love should be easy to get. All we have to do is reach out to others, touch their hands physically, touch their hearts verbally. It's like priming a pump—putting in water starts the well flowing. It's the same with people. Give some love and it will start flowing back to you. When another person opens up, reveals his feelings, who among us can refuse to respond? Yet so many of us find it difficult to open up and ask for the love we desperately want.

I think any couple who has slept together has experienced this scenario at least once: You're both angry, you're both hurt, and you find your way to the same bed—the bigger the better. Thank God, in this instance, for the king-sized version. You're on your side, and she's on hers. There is a vast desert between you. You want nothing more than to be close, to hold her. She wants the same, but neither one dares utter a word. Then a foot, it doesn't matter whose, slowly transverses the width of the bed and "accidently" touches the foot of the other person. In its own right, it's an act of reaching out, an attempt at reconciliation. You are fully aware of what it represents, yet one of you pushes the foot away with the mild force to a verbal rejection: "Leave me alone!" The game has started, but neither one of you can risk winning by openly verbalizing your desire or emotions.

Isn't it interesting that winning in this situation means opening up, sharing emotions, but that it would be perceived as losing? It is sad that we were never taught that losing battles can win the war. Loving entails letting down our guard so people can get close if they choose. It becomes important for each of us to realize that in the course of life, our goal—to get love, to have meaningful relationships with others—is possible if we are really willing to let go, to reveal ourselves honestly.

Honesty in our interactions requires us to pay attention to what is going on in our lives, to have the courage to look at the long-standing patterns of behavior we use. Lack of emotional honesty isn't always apparent to us and operates in an insidious way. An inability to recognize our inner feelings makes us unable to share ourselves. Such dishonesty provides the numberless examples of relating that we, once children, were exposed to and learned. At one level of awareness we were disillusioned by what we witnessed. On another level we learned to imitate that style of loving, even though we resisted seeing it in our parental figures.

Sue Ellen grew up in a home with a doting mother who kept her daughter in pinafores, ribbons, and curls. Sue

Ellen's mother was an aggressive woman who criticized Sue Ellen's father and manipulated the man endlessly. So that he could maintain a so-called loving marriage, her father did anything her mother requested. In Sue Ellen's own words, he would come home from a hard day's work, just lean back in his favorite chair when the phone would ring, and her mother would call, "Dear, would you please get that?" Dad would wearily get up, go to the other room, and answer the phone only to respond, "It's for you, honey."

Each time Sue Ellen heard him say "honey," her insides tightened. She wished, just once, that he would yell, "Get your own damn phone! I am not your servant!" Her father never did that. Sue Ellen grew up feeling love and compassion toward him, but she was also contemptuous and critical of his dishonesty.

What became normal for Sue Ellen in a loving situation was what she learned from the interplays among her mother, her father, and herself. Thus, when she grew up she had learned two roles in loving relationships: She could be the pretty, delicate little girl, eternally compliant, or she had the capacity for being a demanding, controlling, strong-minded individual like her mother, who insisted that others meet her needs. Sue Ellen learned to do anything but go after love honestly, with an awareness of the ways she handled getting love.

Just as Sue Ellen, we all develop the capacity to play more than one role in our relationships as we grow up. While playing roles we become insensitive to our own feelings. But even when we *are* aware of them, we accept extreme contradictions between what we feel and what we do. If we play the obedient role that most people learn as children, we dislike ourselves. When we act as the domineering parent, we have little respect for those who allow us to dominate them. It takes great self-acceptance to see the reality of our behavior. We become defensive and give rationalizations to justify our actions. We do anything but view them honestly and accept them. And yet if we are ever to be liberated enough to find real love, we must go through the step of owning up to what we do and what we feel.

So Sue Ellen has to think back to the time her boyfriend was lying in the hospital very ill and totally preoccupied with whether he would ever be able to work again. She cannot forget how she confronted his physical weakness and inattention. "Do you know how much I have given you in the past weeks?" she demanded. "Do you know how much I have tended to you and cared for you?" In a moment the sweet, agreeable little girl was gone, replaced by the cold, controlling mother who stormed, "But do you realize how little you've given me?" Each time Sue Ellen recalls this, she cringes and wants to forget and deny her spoiled behavior. I want her to comprehend that we must remember our patterns. Certainly it was hard for Sue Ellen to look back upon her insensitivity in the face of her boyfriend's fear and pain and be able to laugh at herself, but that's what I've suggested she do. I've said, "See yourself, standing there in the hospital, and (let's exaggerate now) picture him in casts, traction, totally incapacitated, with his arms and legs dangling from pulleys. Your standing over him and demanding, 'Now, listen, I've given you enough. It's time for you to raise up and give me a hug!' And laugh."

Sometimes the things we do are ridiculous. Perhaps pathos is a more accurate word to describe the mixture of humor and sadness that results as we become aware of ourselves. If we cannot see the humor in our controlling behavior, how can we ever accept ourselves and feel good enough about what we are despite what we do? How can we have the courage to go on in life and alter the way we interact with people we care for?

An old adage comes to mind, "Laugh and the world laughs with you. Weep and you weep alone." It behooves us to look at how many times we have actually chosen to cry alone because we were unable to face the truth about our love. There we were, confined in a jail behind walls of our own making. No wonder we have found it difficult to laugh. Who can laugh when they feel deprived of their freedom and controlled by others around them?

There stood Sue Ellen at her lover's bedside unable to love and unable to feel loved because she was ruled by the roles she had learned, roles it hurt too much to confront. Sometimes we can achieve an honest approach to love by emotionally extricating ourselves from our immediate dilemma. All we need is to step back sufficiently far enough from ourselves to see how we are acting in our own peculiar fashion. Then we can at least smile at ourselves. On other occasions, we can be aided by friends who know us—that is, if they are willing and confident enough of our friendship to be honest with us and indicate how foolish our actions really appear.

For my entire life I will remember an incident that occurred when I first went into private practice. At the time I was working at what seemed four or five jobs. My wife was teaching and taking care of two small children as well as our household. Our schedules barely overlapped, and we rarely saw each other. As a consequence, I frequently found myself arriving home to a dimly lit house and a plate of food warming in the oven. During one particular stretch when I was feeling overworked, unappreciated, and needing someone to take special note of my endeavors, I began to complain—but not openly, mind you. That would have been too simple and too revealing. Instead,

I mentioned that I was coming home to rather skimpy meals. I also noted that no one was up when I arrived home, despite the fact that it was typically after eleven. I suggested that somehow my wife was falling down on the job. It would have been so easy for her to have taken the bait. Can you picture it? She could have pointed out the food in the oven, how hard she worked, how little time I was giving to her and the kids. She could have pointed out that she worked too, and that she had rights also. Instead, Harriet waited for just the right moment. I arrived home several nights later to a totally dark house. I walked through the front doorway and suddenly lights flooded the dining room. A table laden with food stood before my eyes, the candlelight glowed. And there stood my wife, dressed as if she were ready for a formal ball, complete with a rose between her teeth. I was aghast. I thought, "What do I do now?" I was already tired and dragging. I was no more able to enjoy sitting at a formal table with candlelight and china than I would have been able to fly. Suddenly the total ludicrousness of the situation became so apparent. I had been a fool! There was no way to do anything but laugh at the situation, at my wife standing there, in her evening gown, and most important, at myself. It's nice to have someone love and accept you, but it's even better when you acknowledge and accept yourself.

Too often, we are afraid to ask honestly for the love we want. All of us will face the emotional trap of attempting to get love by rules we learned as children. Irv, even though he loves a good laugh, sometimes takes his feelings too seriously. For example, one night he arrived at his girlfriend's to find a specially cooked meal of liver and onions. He should have felt great pleasure at this special treat, but he knew that liver is a dish she doesn't like. Consequently, although he felt pleased, his pleasure was not complete. "Well, are you going to have some?" he asked. As he expected, her answer was, "No. You know I don't like it. I'll eat something else." Irv felt disappointed because he had learned early in life that loving is not only doing something for somebody but also sharing in the enjoyment.

He tried his best to feel bad when Karen refused to share the meal even though his mind said, "Fool! What kind of idiot are you? Look what she did just for you. Enjoy it!" He was caught in the emotional trap of needing her to eat liver to prove her love for him, all the while knowing at another level of awareness that he consciously had to alter his behavior. Consequently he said more than "Thank you." He made himself add, "I know that you don't like liver and onions. This was a really loving, considerate thing for you to do. You're neat." Irv's head believed those words, his mind forced him to say them, and perhaps when he is older and grayer, his stomach—and his feelings—will concur with them. Every once in a while the old feelings still seem to rise up, and I dare say till the day he dies, Irv will have to practice loving in the way he wants to do and not in the way he learned was "normal." He will have to remember that in this instance Karen's intentions and feelings actually were of little consequence. How he interpreted her behavior and reacted to it is important, for each of us interacts with our world in terms of our own perspective and individual realities.

Irv will always backslide, for none of us can so control our behavior that the old, habitual forms of loving won't make themselves known. That isn't necessarily bad, for it is part of who we are. *We must risk letting ourselves and others see both sides of our personality.* Let's say Karen had seen the expression on Irv's face and asked, "What's wrong? Don't you like the way I prepared the liver and onions? You should be delighted!" Then he could have answered, "I am delighted. I love it! It's just that I'm a little crazy. A part of me feels that if you really loved me, you'd not only be eating with me, you'd also like them just as much as I do. I know it's crazy, and thanks for what you did." Wouldn't the honest sharing of these feelings have been a free expression of love?

Once, after voicing these ideas in a speech, I listened to a member of the audience exclaim in utter frustration, "What you advocate sounds so simple, but the minute you finished talking, I had two reactions. First was sort of amnesia that came over me at the end of your lecture. I forgot everything you said to me because whatever it was sounded so damn simple. Well, it isn't! It's hard to live as you suggest! The next thing I felt is anger. I'm angry at you! You're telling me to do something I don't know if I can do. The words sound easy, but being honest, being vulnerable isn't. When I get out there, I'll get scared, I'll be petrified. I'll barely remember what it was I was supposed to do, and then when I finally get it through my head that I'm just supposed to drop my guard and go up to people and reveal myself, I'll be tongue-tied. I wonder what there is in me to reveal to others. I truly don't know which foot to put forward first, let alone what to say."

The work of being honest is hard. The effort to be openly loving doesn't stop after one instance. It must go on and on. *Loving requires constant effort.* I'm not repeating myself because I feel people are incapable of comprehending what I say, but rather because I believe that most of us think that a one-time attempt at altering our behavior is enough. Change demands long-term commitment. In practice that can be harder to accept than it seems.

I once knew a man who had tremendous difficulty in expressing his feelings for his girlfriend. He wasn't able to let her know how he had been hurt by her, how much he cared for her, and he regretted hurting her. He became tremendously frustrated when it was suggested that he tell his girl what was on his mind, how much he wanted her love. He was told that he must express to her how he wished to stop cheating on her and begin involving her in his life. "Do you know how difficult this is to say to her?" he cried. "Will I have to work this hard the rest of my life to make relationships work?" My answer was, "Yes, you are going to have to work this hard always, because the way you learned to go about getting love isn't the way that works. At least it doesn't work to give you the kind of relationship you'd like. You are in the position where, probably for the rest of your life, you will consciously have to put out some effort, day in and day out, to say and do what will obtain the kind of loving relationship you desire." How often people react negatively to that statement. It's as though we believe that having once declared our feelings, we can put them safely away. We're embarrassed and scared of them. My retort has always been that you ate breakfast yesterday, and yet you're hungry this morning. You told someone you loved that person yesterday, and you need to say it again today. You also need to ask for repeated assurances that you are loved in return.

Never stop trying. As long as you're involved, interested in another person, and wish to achieve some level of intimacy with them, you must keep trying to let them know what you feel. When you decide to stop trying, you may as well get out. Arriving at the conclusion that it is no longer worth trying and yet staying in a relationship means that we don't want to have a relationship with anyone. It means we are willing to live dishonestly, maintaining the status quo, something we are willing to settle for most of the time.

To some extent we all think that love will change and be better in the end. We walk around with a silly notion we learned as children: Get yourself locked up in a tower, and your hair will grow to sufficient length to enable a prince to save you; or a fairy godmother will change you from a scullery maid to the princess at the ball within a matter of moments. No matter, eventually we're going to live happily ever after. But that notion is an illusion. To be disappointed and not act when we encounter difficulties, when there is no happily ever after, is immature and leads nowhere.

And yet, *loving honestly doesn't have to be complicated.* We make love into a mystical process with deep, secret rituals that must somehow be learned before we can experience love. But love is right at our fingertips, right within our grasp. *Loving honestly begins with accepting ourselves and our patterns as normal but knowing when not to take them too seriously.* Through honesty, we will obtain the love that keeping a stiff upper lip never got us. Maybe then we will commit ourselves to a mature attempt at loving.

Whenever we create and build anything of value, we also have to concern ourselves with maintaining it. *With interpersonal relationships, the maintenance goes on forever.* When we cry out, "When will it end?" the answer is, "Never." I suspect we'll always have to clean up or paint the walls, even in heaven, if we want them to be clean and bright. *Loving demands honest and constant effort—and a sense of humor.* It also demands realism; fairy-tale endings don't happen to real human beings. We have to work at love. But it's worth the effort, because good relationships and comfortable, happy environments are worth our conscious endeavor.

CHAPTER 10

Vulnerable Love: Using Pain Positively

I have a dear friend who had tried suicide and was on drugs. For a long time, when he was in the throes of his painful experiences, he would come over and grab hold of me on a Sunday morning and we would sit and talk. Once, while in the depths of his depression, he cried, "I don't understand it. I've known you all these years. We've been around together, and you never get depressed, you never feel bad. Why not?"

I shook my head. "You are absolutely wrong," I answered. "Of course I feel bad. Of course I really hurt. I have heartaches that just tear me up inside."

"Well, what do you do about them? Because I wind up drinking, or smashing myself with drugs. Sooner or later I collapse, depressed, unable to function. What do you do?"

"I enjoy it."

"You're telling me you're masochistic, you like to hurt?"

"No. I profit from the pain. I learn from distress. I grow because of it in one way or another. I discover where the hurt is coming from, and that enables me to learn how to

deal with what I find out about myself. I learn how to eliminate the pain or perhaps simply to accept its presence.

At the time he couldn't understand what I meant, and I
really could find no further way to explain how I use pain
in my life. Only sometime later, as I was talking to another
friend, did I hit upon the explanation.

There is no way to get up any morning of your life and
live a whole day in which you are not confronted by some
problem, whether it be how to pay for unexpected car re-
pairs or how to find someone to love you. As long as we
live we will sometimes feel trapped, inundated; feel that,
like Henny Penny, the sky is falling on us. All of that is
painful.

But there are two kinds of pain. The first kind is any
distress that can make me change for the better. Pain that
leads to change is valuable pain. I have learned that this
positive pain I experience in life comes from what I see
and realize and dislike about myself. There are times when
I see myself not confronting people who are intimidating.
I observe myself backing down, giving in, and at those
times I almost hate myself. It is the resulting stab of self-
dissatisfaction that causes me to decide I've got to alter my
behavior. That's productive pain.

Negative pain is different. It is pain that does nothing
more than hurt. It's like the illness of a hypochondriac
who can't afford to get better. His literal aches and pains
serve him in important ways. Surrounded by his veil of
physical preoccupation, he never has to look at the world
around him: He is able to control others and obscure his
own better qualities. His anguish is really designed to op-
erate as a smoke screen from reality.

We use negative pain as a kind of personal pseudo-
therapy. It is a false source of treatment for ills we don't
want to confront, and it masks the real distress we feel in

our relationships. Let me describe what I mean. A personable young man feels too shy to approach relationships with women. Rather than face his problem, he invents a new one. He becomes a dedicated social drinker. To this man such overindulgence is "therapeutic" because it helps him feel more at ease in those situations where available women are present.

Much unproductive pain resolves around "harmless" little habits that drive people away. Take constant indecision about where you would like to go on a night out. Even if it causes arguments, it is easier to turn the decision over to someone else than to look at yourself and investigate why you can't make up your mind. Of course, you live with the incessant worry that other people will become so exasperated they'll call it quits with you.

Still, it could be easier to have trouble making decisions than to tell the truth, that you feel intimidated by the people you need in your life. It can be hard to admit that you are too dependent and afraid of losing love or discovering that you can't make it through life without someone to guide you.

We use much of the negative pain we experience as a defense mechanism. As such it becomes an ingrained behavioral syndrome which persists. Because it is a mechanism for coping, we rationalize its place in our lives rather than give it up. Witness the woman who loudly and frequently berates her man. We feel uncomfortable around her abusive criticism and wonder that she cannot soften her comments with a little kindness. Obviously she is not happy with her relationship, but she defends herself by stating that such honesty is the basis for her love.

We live under the illusion that our defensive behaviors are beneficial, but such mechanisms only prolong our wretchedness. So why do we hold on to them?

These defenses, painful though they are, help us avoid wrestling with the real source of our pain, the potential for being hurt in our search for love.

Even when they hurt, our defenses enable us to hide inner reality from ourselves and others in the world. That reality is the fear that we *might* be rejected, *might* be hurt by someone we care for, *might* not be enough to merit a return of the love we offer. At some level of awareness any pain seems more bearable than the exposure of these fears and hurts, which lie deep inside every one of us.

So it is that the young man avoids facing his fear of women through painful drinking. The woman who criticizes her lover doesn't have to look at what angers her in herself, her own uncomfortable sense of inadequacy. And my friend's anguish, his spells of depression, the overwhelming despair he endures because of his addiction, doesn't reach as deep as his fear of relating and dealing with people. These people can't afford to give up their negative pain. That's why my friend can't get rid of the drugs. If taking drugs hurts that much, he'd stop, but the pills mask the pain he can't face, the pain of feeling vulnerable before people he needs and loves.

The many mechanisms we use day in and day out are no less effective at concealing our real anguish than my friend's drug addiction. The daily avoidance of our own personal reality, the reality of the pain entailed in loving are sometimes just more subtle, that's all. It requires great inner perception to see what's really going on within us, even more to recognize that we stage our own peculiar kind of painful circumstances and then live as victims.

> We enter into relationships where we will be controlled and disappointed and then suffer because we are frightened to risk being rejected.

We flinch under a partner's anger when much of it would be dissipated had we followed up on promises we made to them.

We have an affair with a married person and are in misery because they are not available rather than face the deeper anxiety of dating a man or woman who is.

The better our use of negative pain has worked, the more difficult it is to get rid of. The more effective our means of avoiding positive pain, the harder it is to search for a more rewarding way to face the blows we might experience in trying to love.

When we finally tire of cares that never improve, misery that doesn't end, heartaches that lead nowhere but back to the same rut we are always in, then we are finally forced to ask, "What's wrong with me? What's going on in me?" We can postpone these questions. We can even block the exquisite, traumatic pain that is present in our lives, especially that which might have begun when we were the extra child, the displaced child, the lonely or ignored child, even the overindulged, emotionally protected child. Sooner or later, however, we have the chance to give up our negative pain, which only keeps us from loving.

Facing who we really are and the causes for our pain can be devastating at first. The man who confronts the illusion that his was a happy childhood when it was not is now going to feel the sorrow he tried to avoid as a child. Coming to grips with the source of his loneliness today opens up his world to a loving life tomorrow. Certainly this was true for Blake. The son of a country minister, his early life was emotionally and financially deprived. His parents were preoccupied with their church activities and responsibilities. Blake was cared for mainly by his other siblings. Now in his early fifties, Blake has often wondered about his childhood, which he vaguely remembers, and he recently asked his older sister what happened to him upon the birth of their youngest brother. She responded, "You became a leftover. The family's attention was completely diverted from you to him."

His sister's comments resurrected the indelible pain of those years for Blake, but they have finally explained for him the source of the emptiness and sense of rejection that has haunted him all his life. Neither his several marriages nor his financial successes have helped him escape that pain. They only added to it. His sister's words forced him to accept this distressing reality.

Such discoveries hurt, but it is *positive* hurt because it is therapeutic. It is therapeutic because it spurs growth in the ability to seek out love. This growth begins when a person says, "I recognize this about myself, and I don't like it. I am hurting so badly that I've got to change my behavior." That statement constitutes facing reality. And yet the admission alone is not enough to make our pain productive. Seeing ourselves, faults and all, doesn't change us. So why make the effort to understand ourselves and what we are actually feeling?

The benefit of understanding ourselves is learning that we need not be emotionally crippled by the pain of our reality. The positive pain that results from seeing ourselves is the impetus for the kind of changes in our lives that will let us experience real love.

For instance, I always thought Fitz was just naturally the life of the party. But when I got to know him better, I understood that he was driven to be a good-time-Charlie as a way to conceal his own pain. Fitz tells me that when he was a kid and got hurt in this rough-and-tumble world, he did several things to ease and prevent further pain. He talked on and on, albeit brilliantly, about any topic. And he told jokes. Fitz knew all the latest anecdotes and he was funny, but few people ever got past the laughing exterior to see what was really going on.

"Whenever I felt dumb I could come out with a funny line. Whenever I felt inadequate or threatened I talked so much that people dubbed me the Philadelphia lawyer." Fitz wisely came to realize that his joking and talking are signposts to alert him that he is either feeling bad or inadequate.

Most recently, he and his wife joined three other close couples for dinner, when someone made the mistake of asking Fitz about his tennis game. Fitz launched into a monologue that was humorous, entertaining, and very, very lengthy. When his wife later mentioned that he had dominated much of the conversation that night while commenting at length on his backhand, Fitz retorted that he had been bright, brilliant, uproariously funny. Why worry? Nobody lost. Or had they? No one remarked about his behavior, they seemed to have had a good time, the party broke up in good spirits. Yet he felt close to none of his dinner companions. None of them had seen the real Fitz.

Fitz realized that he had succumbed to a very old behavior of his and that something must have been bothering him. He has learned that such behavior is his means of curing the old feeling of inadequacy he sometimes experiences. His domination of the evening's conversation concealed his depression over a major problem encountered while building a new home and the ineffectual ways he had dealt with the builder.

Once he was aware of that, Fitz went to his wife and said, "I really feel terrible. That's why I joked so much last night. I need you. I need your love." He also chose to share with his friends what was going on so they could know how he really felt. It hurt deeply to acknowledge his regressive behavior and to admit his limitations, but it was a positive hurt. It was not a false attempt to cope but a chance to open up, to grow.

Once we recognize that pain is a part of life, we can begin to look for the pain beneath the pain and get down to the real source of our misery. There is no need to fight the pain, only to learn from it. Experiencing the real pain of our inadequacy need not make us any less able to be ourselves. Fitz still jokes and laughs, but that recent gathering reminded him that sometimes it is better to face what is really happening and to share the reality with others he loves. Joking at such a time brings him neither love nor hate, but sharing his feelings does. It is the only possible way to get love. From Fitz we can learn quickly all the steps needed to turn our pain into a positive experience for growth.

- Recognize that there is no way to experience life without experiencing pain and that this pain need not hinder loving. Positive pain can be used to aid the search for love.
- Discover the ways you obscure the pain of facing yourself. In Fitz's case it is to joke and talk incessantly.
- Use your pain as a signpost to tell you when you're feeling bad. In this way it can serve as a form of personal insight.
- Ask someone you trust and love to help make you aware of the times you attempt to cover up your inadequacies by using old behaviors. Risk opening up; become vulnerable.
- Learn that loving someone else needn't trap you: You needn't sell yourself short, lie, or behave out of obligation rather than desire.
- Know that only when you face your pain can you conquer your inner fears and realize that you are worthy of love.

There are very practical ways to utilize these steps effectively. They involve taking responsibility for the unhappy situations in our lives. I know we can, as people do, play the "if only" game:

- If only my kids were different, I would feel better.
- If only my wife treated me differently, I could love her more.
- If only my boyfriend weren't traveling all the time, I would feel more loved.
- If only my husband came home and talked more, I'd feel we had a better marriage.

I agree with all the excuses people can offer. But other people are not the basic reasons we feel unhappy. Ninety-five percent of the time, we feel unhappy not because of what is going on in our world, but rather because of how we *deal with* what is going on in our world. We can be in touch with ourselves, and at the same time people still can make us feel bad—but only insofar as we let them.

Most of us would prefer to feel that our problems stem from someone else and from conditions outside our control. We would like to believe that our unhappiness comes from the fact that we are trapped in our marriages, our jobs, our families; that we owe our heartaches to our responsibilities, our debts, the pressures of the world. And that there is nothing we can do about it. I share this tendency. When I feel unhappy, the last thing I want to do is examine myself and conclude, "Ed Reitman, it's you who are responsible." But if ever I am going to do more than protect myself while living with a great deal of pain, then I must find a way to cope with and to resolve whatever situation I find myself in. I have to remind myself that, like everybody else, I feel bad 95 percent of the time not because I am controlled by others or trapped by circumstance but because I am controlled and trapped by my own fears.

We have the option of trying to avoid the real pain of that realization and thereby creating negative, nonproductive pain; or we can choose to deal with the thorny issues that await us every morning as we step out of bed. We make that task seem difficult and complex, but again the solution is simple: Do what makes us feel good about ourselves.

Do I feel bad because I am overweight? If that is true, then I can choose to feel good. Stop eating. Or exercise. Or see a doctor to determine the cause. If I don't, then I must want to feel bad for a reason. My desk is piled with all kinds of paperwork. Every time I sit down to it, I look at the stacks of work and become totally despondent. Do I want to feel good? Clean it up. If I don't, I must want to feel bad for a reason. And if I am having an affair and I feel so guilty that it tears me up inside, then I can stop it. Unless maybe I need to feel bad. Unless it helps me to avoid looking at myself and how afraid I am to open up to my mate.

Do you want to eliminate some of the burdens you bear? You now have the means. You can't change anything in other people. But you can start dealing differently with them and with the situations that arise around you. It's not one grand, glorious change that suddenly makes you feel good. It's a parade of little ones that follow the overall decision to do things that make you feel good. This does not mean you do anything that makes you feel good but that you do things that will make you feel good about yourself in retrospect. You confront the problems you didn't create and decide how you will handle them. You take the risk of experiencing the positive pain that you cannot avoid if you want to live and love realistically. You face the negative, sad feelings and the feeling of being trapped because you know the trap comes from the fear within. The child may turn away, the lover may reject you, and the spouse may never be sympathetic. But there can be joy in that painful coming to grips with the risks and the fears of emotional honesty. It is the joy of being reborn into a world where real love is possible. It is the joy in the kind of pain long-distance runners endure as they near the goal. It is the sense of growth and the opportunity for new love that is our reward for choosing positive pain.

CHAPTER 11

Discerning Love: Finding New Friends

About three years ago, a patient of mine who was going through a divorce shared with me a record of her progress through therapy, which was really her progress in learning how to love. One notation in her diary was especially significant because it describes the kind of awareness we all encounter once we commit ourselves to the pursuit of real love.

> Today is August 8. I am thirty-one years old. . . . It is very hard struggling out of this cocoon of my past years. There is so much fear and anxiety. I don't always know what I should do or even what I want to do. I try to take a day at a time but sometimes it seems that time is slipping through my fingers. This causes me to worry and feel anxious. I worry that these feelings will make me move too fast and move into situations that I am not ready for.
> I do not want to hurt or be hurt. I am

> suspicious of all those around me. There
> are so many games played by so many, and
> I feel inadequate because I don't know the
> games or the rules. I do not know what to
> expect, so I try not to expect anything. I
> think there will be less pain that way. At the
> same time, I'm afraid that this attitude will
> keep me from what I want.
>
> I do not like being alone. I hate it. It hurts
> me and makes me feel angry and afraid. I
> feel alone so much, even when I am with
> others. I wish I knew how to make friends.

Kathy, my patient, had arrived at the inevitable moment of uncertainty that comes when we decide to give up those patterns of behavior that offer only fraudulent love.

In a sense, it is like giving up old friends—not necessarily good friends, but the kind of friends who have been around a long time and who are comfortable to be with simply because they have been around so long. It is frightening to think that it is these friends, these destructive behaviors, that hurt us most. We keep them around so we can control our lives and therefore keep from getting hurt. Because of the way we've grown up, because of the way we were trained, because of the way others have taught us to look at life, all of us—and there are no exceptions—have learned that love is control.

A favorite friend for many people is guilt. Witness the woman with the deep sighs, the rolling eyes, the person who interrupts you with, "Excuse me while I take the pill my doctor gave me today." Guilt is her friend and she employs it freely, unconsciously, hoping that it will ensure her loyalty and love from those around her. But look closer to see what these moralistic kind of manipulations gain her— an insidious kind of power that ultimately drives others away. Her family may wait on her, they may call daily to say, "Mother, is your back getting better?" but they are never really able to love her or receive her love in return because they are controlled by guilt.

There are many ways to control. Each of us has a different style, different friends. To find out which is yours, ask yourself what you do when you get upset. Do you go home and go to bed? Do you get physically sick and suffer from headaches? Do you light up another cigarette or order one more drink? Maybe you take a pill, or help yourself to one more serving, or maybe you have sex promiscuously. Perhaps you get angry and go on bombastic tirades, or maybe you're the opposite, acquiescing like a sweet little child who is dependent and helpless. All of these are our reactions to bad feelings about ourselves; they are our way of controlling others and defending ourselves.

Terri is a woman I have been seeing in therapy for the last six months. Years ago, I saw her husband Dick, on a regular basis, but Terri started coming in because she was suicidal, completely depressed. Today, her depressions are shorter, but acute nevertheless. Lately they revolve around a pretty young blonde who works with Terri and Dick in their office. This is a woman Terri hired herself, yet scarcely three weeks after the woman reported to work, Terri found herself intensely jealous of her. This woman is twenty-five years younger than Dick and very attentive to him, bringing in the morning coffee and running helpful little errands. She has no hesitation about walking into Dick's office at any time. She feels comfortable asking him what he needs and offering letters for him to sign. Terri is upset because, even as Dick's wife, she has always felt reluctant to intrude on his privacy for fear of disturbing him and making him angry. She has always been hesitant to bring him her problems for fear he would demand to be left alone.

Curiously, when the young blonde announced that she might be leaving in a few weeks to take a better job, Terri could not stand to see her go. The very thought of it threw her into another depression. She even went to her husband and appealed to him to give the girl a raise in hopes it would change her mind. The blonde got the raise but she never got the other job she interviewed for, so she remains doing the same job for a higher salary at no more competent a level than before. Now Terri is really depressed.

I told Terry, "If that girl bothers you day in and day out, get rid of her and hire someone else." But she protested.

"You don't know how much she does! If she leaves, you can't imagine how much work will be on my back."

None of this was true. Terri is an attractive lady, competent in her own right, and she handles a great deal of responsibility in her husband's office. Dick is a professional whiz, but beyond that, he stumbles along. He needs Terri. Terri's jealousy was inappropriate, yet she clung to it. She could not afford for the girl to leave because Terri needed jealousy to cover the real reason for her depression. Jealousy was Terri's friend and she couldn't let it go. What was really bothering Terri was an intense feeling of inadequacy, of fear. Could her husband—or any man, for that matter—love her? As awful as the depression was, as painful as those hopeless, suicidal impulses became, it was worse for Terri to have to face her own fears. Jealousy was the bad friend who guaranteed she would never get a good look at who she really was.

WHO ARE YOUR NEUROTIC FRIENDS?

You can always tell your destructive friends by one thing: They never really help. They may help at first, they may give you the feeling that you're doing better, but not for long. I know who I turn to when I get upset: my friend food. I sit down to a plate of pasta and say to myself, "I'm going to hate you in the morning, Ed Reitman, but I'm going to feel awfully good tonight." Eating that pasta gives me an excuse to look in the mirror and get upset over my weight and ignore those other areas of my life that are really bothering me.

Food is a favorite friend of mine, but I have others, too. If I don't pull out pasta, I'll tell a joke, and if I don't tell a joke, I'll go to work.

Another person's friend might be anger. I've seen people actually recall a child's death to mourn over again. By using the overwhelming sadness surrounding the loss of a child, they can continue to feel horrible about themselves. In fact, they can get attention, even approval, for feeling horrible. By virtue of this tragic experience in their past, they can subtly reject everybody, and nobody would dare blame them for it. But they pay a high price for their friend. When you rely on these destructive defense mechanisms, you end up separating yourself from the very thing you want most, and that thing is love. What you get in its place is loneliness.

It is important for all of us to learn how to identify our neurotic friends so that when they show up in our lives, we can be rid of them quickly. And yet, even when we realize that we must banish these self-destructive behaviors from our lives, even when we know full well that they keep us from getting love and giving it back, even when we feel them coming on and hate ourselves for falling back into the same old patterns of behavior—even then, it is painful to see them go.

But why? Why is it so hard to stop hurting ourselves? There's not a soul in this world who doesn't need love. There is not one of us who is not hungry for human involvement. The problem is, we don't really feel that we're worthy of the love we want so much, and we're frightened of the possible rejection we are going to experience if anybody knows we need love.

I know a woman who feels she must be a martyr in order to feel worthy of being loved. She packs the trunks three times for her sister-in-law's moves, then she delivers the furniture. For this she receives no thanks, yet at the first opportunity, she is there doing it all over again. She cooks dinner for her friends without a word of thanks and, of course, she never gets the appropriate display of gratitude for being the best mother and the hardest-working secretary, either. The fact that she is a martyr is not the important thing, because her selfless suffering is only a symptom. It is the illness that I care about, the abiding ailment that convinces her and the rest of us that we are not really worth loving or that loving costs too much. It is our avoidance of these deep-rooted feelings that keep us trapped in repetitious and self-defeating behavior and prevent us from getting the love we want.

When we decide to give up these friends we feel awkward, as if we are not sure what is going on. It is not easy to give up unproductive behaviors and find new ways to express our feelings. Intellectually, I know what causes us the problem. We need other people, but we want them without getting hurt. *This is impossible.* If you want love, you cannot get it without being hurt. The critical stage occurs when you decide to make the break, to risk the pain by dropping those behaviors. After that, miracles don't happen, because none of us can change completely, but we can change in some very significant, encouraging ways, as exemplified by the experience of a couple I see in therapy.

Marge is a woman with a short fuse, little self-confidence about her ability to be loved, and a person who equates love with gifts. Frank is a man who uses money to control. Every time she needs love, she asks him to buy her something. The only way he feels loved is to know he is in control and has power over her. The power comes from having money. He answers her wheedling for this and that by going into his routine. "Are you out of your mind? We can't afford that! I'm expanding the office, I'm hiring four new employees. Don't be ridiculous!"

This sort of wrangling had been the story of their marriage until a few weeks ago. The situation turned out differently this time.

They were having their usual argument, this time over a wristwatch Marge wanted. Things went on this way, off and on for days, until the night Frank got drunk and made the promise to buy his wife a Rolex with diamonds. Naturally, when he sobered up, he had a change of heart. The following month was filled with arguments about making promises that aren't kept. At any rate, as a concession on her part, Marge said she would settle for a simple little gold watch with only a few diamonds on the face. The whining was renewed and so were the refusals, until a week before her birthday. Then Frank came up with an idea he felt was guaranteed to hook her for good.

"You can have the watch," he promised, "but you are going to have to sign a contract saying you will not ask me for another thing for the next two years." Then he proceeded to draw up the document and hand it to his wife for her signature. Instead of becoming hysterical the way she would have in the past, she coolheadedly insisted she would not sign it "until my psychologist sees it first." What she wanted, she said, "is for him to look it over and advise me whether he thinks it is worth signing."

When Frank questioned why she would demand such a thing, Marge explained: "Well, if I had a lawyer I would ask him if I should sign a legal document. This is an emotional document, so my therapist should counsel me on it."

Almost at once Frank decided his proposal was not such a good idea after all, and he pulled it back from her.

"Now, wait a minute," she assured him. "Don't get me wrong. I'm willing to sign. I just want my adviser to recommend what I should do. If you are too embarrassed to have him see this, then maybe there is something wrong with it." Suddenly Frank laughed self-consciously. The ruse was up. "Never mind," he said with a wave of his hand. "A verbal contract is just as good as a written one." The next day they went to the jewelry store together and purchased the gold watch. More important, Frank was even able to say a day or two later how happy he was to give it to her. Because Marge was finally able to stand up to Frank, and because he was finally able to cease using money as a control over his wife, an old cycle had been broken at last.

Imagine the benefits if only you could go about breaking your destructive patterns even 65 percent of the time. Or imagine being honest with yourself half the time. That's not much to aim for. The rest of the time you may continue to slip into old patterns, but these will be less destructive because more often you'll be letting someone else know you for who you really are.

Giving up old friends doesn't mean you give up pain. It is a matter of putting yourself in a position where you can be hurt far more than ever before in your life but one in which you're going to like yourself more than you ever have, because you have a self to like. Little by little, the fear diminishes as well.

CHAPTER 12

Healthy Love:
Starting
Where It Began

"**I**s that all there is?"

If you have ever asked yourself this question, then you are probably one of those people who has somehow felt cheated in life, who has sensed there is something missing, a key to life and lasting relationships you have searched for but never found.

If you want to add new vigor to all your relationships, you must first recognize how you were first taught to love. For each of us, our initial contact with love was through our mothers. We learned to love not specifically according to the way our mother loved, but rather by fitting into the scheme of loving behavior between mother and father and between mother and us.

Inevitably, people say, "My mother wasn't there," or "She died," or "I was an orphan and lived with someone else." It makes no difference if you never knew your biological mother or if she did not raise you. The fact is, you are a human being and you learned to love from someone. Perhaps the surrogate mother was a father or a grandmother, maybe an aunt or an uncle. Even the remembrance of a mother who deserted you can provide the earliest memory of a pattern of loving that you were exposed to and later incorporated into your own concept of what love should be.

The game of love we learned early in life compares with the moves we make when we play a hand of bridge. In bridge, you don't play one role. You must learn how to deal, how to bid, how to be a dummy, and how to be a good opponent. Your ability to play the game of bridge is based on your ability to play each of these roles. In the game of love, you must also move from one role to another. We can play the role of a child; we can play the loving role that we first saw in Mother. We can also play the role that we first saw in Father when he interacted with Mother. Likewise, when we choose a spouse, when we relate with our children, when we interact with our friends, our unconscious mind cleverly allows us to adjust to the roles we play.

In no way am I trying to suggest that your mother is a bad person, an evil being who is the cause of all your problems. I am only saying that she knew how to love in accordance with the rules she learned from her mother, from the example of love she observed in her own family. If those were the only rules she knew, then it follows that those were the only rules she could impart to you. If you want to change the way you deal with your husband, your wife, your lover, your children, your co-workers and friends, then you must go back to your mother and change the way you deal with her. You must establish a new loving pattern to get all the love you always wanted but somehow never received. If your mother is no longer alive, you can still return to the other important people in your life and establish a new foundation on which to base your love.

Whenever I think of a man returning to his mother for love, I think of Jack. He was the kind of man who had gone through life unconsciously striving for mediocrity. Because he was bright and capable, he found himself on the verge of success many times, yet in the end, success was the elusive state that always seemed just out of his reach.

He grew up in a home where financial success was highly valued. To Jack, success meant money, and money meant love. When his father refused to foot the entire bill for his college education, Jack felt that he was also refusing to love him. When Jack's parents refused to give him a nest egg with which to begin a new business, Jack felt that they were not supporting him, not loving him. All of his opinions of love were based on how many dollars he received, how much they financially supported him. In order to avoid the possibility that his parents might ever hurt him again, he allowed anger and resentment to become his neurotic friends. After several weeks of therapy, he made the decision to call his mother and straighten out their long-ailing relationship.

"Mom," he said, "I don't want to live in the past anymore. I am no longer interested in what happened back there. I haven't called to get angry. I don't want any part of the anger and hostility that has been such a big part of our relationship. What I want from you is love. What I need is your love, and the thing I would like from you more than anything in the world is to hear you say, "Jack, I love you."

Mother responded in the way that you might expect. "Well, of course I love you, Jack. What in the world would ever make you think I didn't?" Jack hung up the receiver somewhat disappointed but nevertheless proud that he had said what he had always wanted to say, even though his mother seemed to miss the point entirely. Several weeks later, Jack received a phone call from his mother. In the past, a call from Mother was always a signal that there was a problem, so it was not unusual that Jack greeted her by saying, "Mom, what's wrong? Why are you calling? Is somebody sick?"

Her answer was a refreshing surprise for Jack. "There's nothing wrong," his mother assured him. "It is just one of those times when I was thinking of you. I only wanted to call to tell you that I love you."

Jack was overwhelmed with joy, with a feeling of warmth and a certain feeling of vulnerability. He didn't know what to do next. He fished for words, but they were not there. He was simply unable to respond. The new rules he had learned for loving escaped him, so he immediately fell back into the old patterns he and his mother had established long ago.

"Uh, I'm glad you called, Mom," he said self-consciously. "I know you'll be happy to hear that I am doing much better on my job. Last month I earned more money than I ever made before. I can already tell that next month will be even better." Just as Jack had fallen back into the old patterns of loving, so did his mother. She responded by saying, "That's good, Jack. I always knew you could do it." He could almost feel her maternal hand patting the top of his head. "I always knew how bright you were." It was just like old times, the bad times. Mother was measuring Jack's personal worth against his ability to earn money. How much more satisfying that contact would have been if my patient had allowed those true feelings of warmth to surface in words.

"Mom," Jack could have said, "you don't know what this call means to me. I feel closer to you right now than I have since I was a little boy. Your calling me and telling me this is what I've wanted to hear from you all my life. It's the kind of love that says you care for me whether I am performing well on the job or not. This phone call tells me that you love me no matter what. Thank you."

Sometimes we can develop new patterns of loving through seemingly simple situations which offer the opportunity to change the whole scope of a relationship. Such an occasion occurred for my patient, Sandra. The message that this young woman always received from her mother was, "I am going to tell you what to do and how to do it, and as long as you behave accordingly, then I am going to love you and be there for you." As a result, Sandra became the classic "good girl." Even at twenty-eight, she was still living by her mother's rules. The only problem was, Sandra resented it greatly. All the positive and healthy feelings she had for her mother were poisoned by her own anger. A chance visit from her parents during the course of therapy provided her with the ideal opportunity to establish a more honest relationship with her mother.

The moment Mother arrived, she began playing her part of the old love game. Sandra had a one-bedroom apartment, and the plan was for her parents to sleep in her room while she bedded down on the living-room couch.

"Honey," Mother suggested, "why don't I help you pull the cot out of the closet? You will be much more comfortable sleeping there than on the couch."

"That's O.K., Mom," Sandra assured her. "I like the couch just fine. There's no need to get out the cot. Lots of nights when I am working late, I just fall asleep on the couch, and it really feels good. I like it, really I do."

Mom came back stronger. "Sandra, I insist! Maybe your father and I should pack up and go to a hotel, because I really can't bear to put you out in this way."

This is where Sandra began changing the rules of the

game. "All right, Mom," she said calmly, "if you want to go to a hotel, then go ahead. The bed in my room will be empty because I intend to sleep on the couch, but I can't stop you from going to a hotel. The bed is there for you if you decide to use it." Needless to say, her mother capitulated and slept in the bedroom.

Sandra was proud of the way she handled things. For the first time, she felt completely adequate and sufficient before her mother. Her self-precept was one of, "I can say what I believe. I can do what I want. I can behave this way." Sandra got what she wanted. Her mother now understood that the old rules of the game no longer applied. But like Jack, Sandra could have taken one more step. She could have said, "Mom, we can fight about this. We can make this terribly difficult for both of us, but it needn't be. Why can't we make it a positive experience? Why can't you see that I love you and I want you here? Why can't you see that I really am old enough to make decisions for myself, that I don't need you to care for me any longer, that the only thing I need from you is your love? Mom, why don't we learn to deal with each other as adults?"

The words themselves are easy, but speaking them, reaching out with all the closeness and vulnerability such intimacy entails, is the difficult part. It is no simple matter to let ourselves get that close to another human being, but it is far easier when we learn and apply the following basic rules to the new game of love we all must learn. These are the themes I have tried to emphasize throughout this book. By applying them, you will find that real loving becomes a more important part of your life.

Make room for the feelings in your life. A man once came to me after seven years of therapy boasting smugly about all the analysis he had received. His understanding of how he got to be what he was was as sophisticated as much of that found in textbooks. Still, for all his superior understanding, this man was in an emotional void. He demonstrated no feelings toward himself or others. This powerful absence affected everything in his life. In business, his self-awareness made him a huge success, but in loving, he was a wretched failure. He was proof that if you cannot feel what you experience, what you see, what you do, then half or maybe more of the great experience of life is absent for you.

This man fought and denied his feelings. Like many of us, he could not recognize the fact that feelings know no rules. Feelings are natural and spontaneous to one's humanness. They are not necessarily socially acceptable, not necessarily socially permissible, but they are there, and to fight them and attempt to control them is a futile expenditure of energy.

There are many people who simply don't know what they feel. They have done such a top-notch job of locking up their feelings that they are unable to differentiate between what they feel and what they think. They use the words "think" and "feel" interchangeably, never recognizing the vast difference between the world of intellect and that of feeling. If you think you have a problem in this area, then look closely at yourself and listen to what you are really saying. During intimate moments, how do you tell the man or woman in your life the way you feel? Even those three potent little words, "I love you," are only a thought until you put feelings behind them.

There is a poignant scene from the famous play *Fiddler on the Roof* where the aging father, Teyve, disarms Golde, his wife of many years, by asking the simple question, "Do you love me?"

"Do I *what?*" she cried indignantly.

"I *said,* 'Do you *love* me?' " he persisted.

"For twenty-five years I have washed your clothes, cooked your meals, cleaned your house, given you children, and milked the cow. After twenty-five years, how can you talk about love?"

Communications suffer when a thinking person attempts to reason the logic of love with a feeling person.

Learn to accept yourself. We may say that we know and like ourselves even when the truth may be that we are scared to death to come face to face with our own naked realities. Often we are reluctant to let others know the real person we are. We play these deceitful games of emotional hide-and-seek because we are terrified that those around us will reject us if we are any other way. If we were to let others catch a glimpse of our raw, inner feelings of inadequacy and insufficiency, then who could really love or like us?

Even so, to live at peace with ourselves, we must learn to accept what we are, even our limitations. Why struggle through life to be a nuclear physicist when you have the capacity to be a fine high-school science teacher? Why fight to get A's when your real limitations might be B's? Why not accept the fact that you may not be a scholar, but instead a worker, and that the ability to work tolerantly with your B intelligence will get you much farther in life than striving to achieve A's, only to be disappointed?

Keep your sense of humor intact. There is no better prescription for good interpersonal relationships than a good sense of humor. If you cannot laugh, then you cannot effectively live and love. People who can't laugh are so preoccupied with defending the small issues of life that they can't see and appreciate the wonderful life we live. One good way to put the troubles of everyday living into proper perspective is to recognize that most of the things we do and say today will be of little concern five years from today. Look back at the things that used to worry you most (if you can even remember them). Are they still of major consequence today?

Peter and Martha experienced a very nasty divorce. They fought madly over children, cars, furniture, bank accounts, and real estate. Peter suffered such intense anger that he couldn't look at Martha without wiping the sweat away. If she was five minutes late delivering the children for an outing, Peter would explode furiously. If Martha asked him to keep the children for an extra thirty minutes while she ran an errand, Peter would refuse out of spite, even though he might have enjoyed spending the time with them.

One day he arrived at Martha's, angry as usual, just waiting for her to pull something else to justify his rage. He rang the bell and waited impatiently. Soon the door was opened and the children ran out noisily. Just as he was getting ready to walk back to his car, he saw Martha's hand rounding the doorway. Her face and body were nowhere in sight, only a patient hand holding a paper plate laden with a huge slice of chocolate cheesecake, about the only thing from Peter's ten-year marriage he had missed. He reached out and took the plate and she closed the door quickly.

So here was Peter balancing his favorite dessert in one hand as he drove down the freeway with two rowdy children in tow, dying all the while to devour the cheesecake but still trying to stay mad at Martha at the same time. He couldn't do it. He envisioned how absurd he must look in such a state, and suddenly he began to laugh uproariously. In the end, humor taught Peter an effective way to deal with a difficult situation. It also taught him that Martha wasn't all bad, either.

Read between the lines of human behavior. It is hard to get the people around you to say what they really mean, what they really feel. Is the woman who insists that she has no interest in clothes telling the truth, or is she really saying, "I look so fat and awful in whatever I wear that I have given up trying to look good in anything"? Is the man who drives an old junker and who claims, "Cars mean nothing to me," really saying, "Since I can't afford to drive the kind of car I like most, I am not allowing myself to enjoy any automobile"?

Ellen was very unsuccessful at reading between the lines of her husband's behavior. Bruce was a building contractor who had just opened a new subdivision. He was promoting it heavily in newspapers and on television, which proved to be an enormous expense, but he had every reason to believe that his dollars would pay off. He then discovered that the tar on his recently paved streets was defective and would not dry. All he could think about were the hundreds of people arriving on the scene who would leave disgruntled after discovering their cars were splattered with tar. Ellen wanted desperately to help him, so she decided to search for ways to help him alleviate the pavement problem. One night soon after, Bruce arrived home from work. Before he could sit down, she proudly presented him with a neatly executed list of four or five different alternatives she had found for remedying the predicament.

To Ellen's dismay, Bruce was livid. He experienced an urge to kill as she efficiently outlined her solutions. He wanted to scream and shout at his wife. "Do you think I'm dumb? Do you think I haven't already come up with the same solutions and ten more on top of those?" He anticipated the beginning of a real explosion, but he caught himself in time. Instead, he was able to say, "If I had wanted to marry a paving engineer, that's what I would have done. When I married you," he said, reaching for her, "what I wanted was a wife, and what I need now is a loving person who can stroke me and tell me that I'm O.K. in spite of this mess." If Ellen had been intuitive enough to read between the lines of Bruce's behavior, she might have seen that when a person is feeling inadequate, helpful solutions often are seen as hostile criticism.

Open up to those around you. Verbal communication is the primary way human beings relate to one another. It simply isn't possible to find the happiness and fulfillment we all want so badly unless we are willing to share our feelings and experiences with others.

Once a man in group therapy explained to the others why he didn't need to share his feelings. "I know I feel inadequate," he said. "I know that I have lots of feelings that people don't know about, but that doesn't mean I have a problem with feelings. It's just that I maintain control over them. The feelings are still there, whether you realize it or not."

The group would not let this man get by with such evasiveness. "It makes no difference what's inside you," a fellow member informed him, "if you can't relate it to us. How can you expect us to guess the way you feel? How can you expect us to care about you if you never let us get to know you?"

All too often, we condemn others for failing to do things we never said we wanted. How many times have you said, "But he should have known that was what I meant"? or, "It doesn't make any difference if I never tell him I love him, he ought to know that by now"?

Sometime ago a young lady I know met a man who was everything she ever dreamed of. He was good-looking, fun to be with, educated, bright, and a successful physician, as well. She was particularly pleased by this relationship because it seemed to be lasting. In the past, she had experienced great difficulty maintaining long-standing commitments with men, but this time it seemed different.

One day he phoned her and asked, "Where do you want to go the next time we get together? Whatever you want to do is fine with me. Just pick the place and I'll take you." She went into a panic. She knew where she wanted to go, but it was a expensive place, and she was afraid that he would think she was the typical money-hungry "princess" men complained about. As a result, when she called him back her conversation went something like this:

"Well, this is where I want to go." She told him. "Is that O.K.?"

"Fine," her date replied. "If you like it, then it's fine with me."

"There's only one problem," she added timidly.

"What's that?"

"Well, it seems there is a seven-dollar cover charge, and I know that's a lot of money, so why don't we go Dutch treat? You pay your way, and I'll pay mine. I would feel better that way."

"Whatever you say. It's all right with me," he agreed.

Inside, she was having a fit. He wasn't supposed to say that! He was supposed to protest, to be indignant that she would even suggest such a thing! She fretted and fumed over this situation until finally one day she called and asked me what I thought she should do.

"What do you want?"

"I want him to take me, and I want him to pay the bill for both of us," she replied firmly.

"Well, why didn't you tell him that in the first place?"

"I was frightened," she admitted. "I was scared. I knew he wouldn't like me if he thought I was after his money."

My advice to her was simple: "Call the man and tell him exactly what you just told me."

She was aghast. "I could never do that!" she claimed.

She did make the call, however, and as you can imagine, things got off to a shaky start. "I decided that I would like you to take me," she said quietly.

"You mean you want me to accompany you?"

"No," she corrected him nervously, "I want you to *take* me."

"Well, that's what I'm going to do. I'm going to *take* you."

Things were getting tough. "Well, that's not exactly what I mean. What I really mean is"—she sputtered—"I'd like you to pay my way, too!" Finally it was out.

"Oh," the man said unconcerned, "you should have said that in the beginning. Sure I will. I'd be glad to."

Consider the difficulty this woman had expressing herself. Think about the multitude of ways she avoided letting him see her for who she really was. It wasn't until she opened up and invited him to look at her feelings that she got what she wanted.

Make a commitment. Human beings must make commitments to something in life. Not only does commitment provide us with direction and motivation, it also gives us a standard by which we can judge our progress in life. If you are committed to something, then that is your goal, and goals are what we need to make our lives meaningful. One commitment most of us end up dealing with one or more times in life is marriage.

Nancy went through a particularly trying time in her marriage. She was an attractive woman who was in the midst of seeking an affair, even though she had a wonderful husband, a man she loved deeply, who, unfortunately, was inadequate sexually.

Nancy was attracted to a handsome young co-worker. She began making involved plans about the way they could meet undetected by either her husband or his wife. She finally called her potential lover and made an engagement to meet him for lunch. In the interim, she asked me, "Should I do it or not?"

"Well, it's your decision," I told her. "What do you want to do?"

"I really want to go through with it," she responded. "It feels good and all week long I've been excited by the thought of seeing him. This is the first time I've been assertive. It's the first time I've ever called him or planned a date. The trouble is, I also want a marriage. I really want it to work, and I really love my husband. I just don't know what to do."

"Well, what is your goal?" I asked.

"I guess my goal is to keep my marriage together."

"O.K," I countered, "you say you want your marriage to work. Simple. Will meeting this man for lunch further your marriage? If a satisfying marriage is your goal, then you have to answer no to that question. But it's your decision." If that wasn't enough food for thought, I gave Nancy something else to consider. "Maybe instead you would like to meet him for lunch to tell him you don't want to see him anymore."

She nodded. "That's a possibility," she admitted.

"You're sadly mistaken if you think that would further your goal of making your marriage work, because if you met this man you would enjoy yourself and probably get excited. You would be sexually stimulated and have all the good feelings associated with an affair, but in the long run it would do anything but benefit your marriage."

Like Nancy, when any of us has a goal, a commitment, we must stand back and judge whether our behavior helps or hinders us in that effort. Meeting this man would require Nancy to come to terms with herself. Is her goal to have an affair, or to break up her marriage? Or is her goal to keep her marriage intact? If she finds that her true goal is marriage, she will have to stop seeing him, even though she doesn't want to, even though it feels good. It's a question of being consistent and realistic. Stopping seeing him doesn't mean an affair itself is right or wrong. I am making no moral judgments here. The desire for an affair may well continue, but Nancy's behavior needs to be determined by her goal, and that is to promote a healthy, happy marital relationship.

The rules for new loving can be frightening because they require a new approach to living. But even in the face of uncertainty, changing, growing, and learning new behaviors are possible for all of us who really want these things. Still, at times many of us begin to wonder if working at such a new way of life is really worth the trouble. The rewards are welcome at any stage in life.

I once knew a man whose wife left him after almost thirty years of marriage. He was hurt, confused, depressed, and angry. He begged her to come back, but she would have no part of him. When I asked why his wife left, he had no answer.

"Go ask her," I suggested. Later he had this answer: "She says I never show feelings. She says I am a cold person." He still didn't understand.

"I tried to explain to her that I never ran around on her. I was home every night for dinner, I never drank too much, and I never hit her." Furthermore, he related defensively, "I made a good living and I provided her with a beautiful home. What more could a woman want?" he asked, throwing his hands toward the ceiling.

"Has anybody else ever said you were a cold person?" I inquired.

"Sort of," he admitted. "One time when I was hunting with a neighbor he said to me, 'You know, if I ever need a heart transplant, I want yours.'"

When I asked what the man meant, my patient lowered

his head and answered quietly, "Because I have never used it myself."

There are many of us who live without our hearts, who are never really able to look within ourselves or at those around us. And yet, why are we alive if not to be who we were created to be? Martin Buber, the renowned theologian and philosopher, exercised thoughtful wit when he wrote of his plans for the afterlife. "When I die and go to heaven, God isn't going to ask, 'Martin, what kind of Moses were you?' He's going to ask, 'Martin, what kind of Martin were you?' "

Ask yourself similar questions: What kind of loving, caring human being are you? How do you want to be tomorrow?

CHAPTER 13

Feeling Love: Winning at Love

You are emotionally at an important moment in your life. You have new insights into the way you've loved all your life, and you know that you want something more from your relationships than you've ever experienced. You are aware of some of the mistakes you've made, and you've also learned new ways to try being intimate. You know you have to be open to love. You have to stand up, have opinions, and be able to speak your mind and express your feelings. Now you should be ready for the last step—the step that says: Here's your chance, starting right now, to obtain the love you missed so often in the past.

The act of going after love is not an ominous, heavy task. It's exciting, challenging, and rewarding. Yet it's not going to be easy. Loving is hard work. It requires vulnerability in the eyes of others and a good deal of critical self-awareness, but it offers its own unique rewards. You can make loving a kind of game in which the only penalty for losing is that you get to try again, as many times as need be, with the increased knowledge gained from your previous attempts. With each successive effort you might ask yourself, "Did I goof up again?" "Did I do it the same way I used to do it?" "Was it the other person's fault?" If your answer is, "I'm afraid I messed it up again," then I would have you promise yourself that, as of right now, you are going to take a couple of minutes extra to share a part of you with every person you meet today who is important to you, whether they be relatives, friends, or business associates. Deliberately take three minutes extra with each individual to show them your concern. Share your feelings and let them know that you really want them as your friend. You might say:

- I like being with you.
- I really feel good knowing you're out there for me.
- I hope you know that you're a very special person in my life.
- It makes me feel very warm and comfortable when we're together.
- I love you and your friendship. You help to make my life extra nice.

Any statement that fits you, that says you care, that you want to love and be loved, will work. It takes that kind of desire and that kind of personal openness to help you love better.

Think about it—if you try with only five people for three minutes each, you will have expended just fifteen minutes extra all day long, but the quality of your day and your relationships could well be enhanced fifteen times over. Even more, you can make loving a personal challenge which proves rewarding and enjoyable. You need only regard each morning as the start of a new day and each relationship, even the oldest one, as novel. Think about getting up in the morning with the notion that you have a wonderful opportunity to improve, build upon, and alter some of the dull, routine relationships you've heretofore neglected or taken for granted. You can make the good ones really good by adding a new wrinkle, a new twist. The bad ones you can improve a little by breaking through someone's wall of indifference. You can insert a new quality into the ones that just exist. You can learn that the possibility of change is exciting.

Enjoy loving! Don't make it an overwhelmingly serious task. Don't look at love in terms of a relationship to end all relationships. Don't think everyone has to be involved with you in this program. Don't worry that if you goof again you'll never change. Instead, think of it as a lifetime process, a game you are never going to perfect completely. Just recognize that every day there is a new chance for you to try again, if just a little bit with only one person. It's all right; a little can be enough. Even more, it can be fun.

Of course, many times your efforts will blow up in your face. But you will have to try again. You must learn that you can strike out in life and still be quite a good person. The only problem is that few of us are willing to risk "flying out" or swinging at air. Too often we won't play the game if we don't think we can win it.

Most of us think only in terms of home runs. Everything we do has to be a total success; it has to come out perfectly or it's unacceptable.

Test yourself to determine to what extent you fall into the category of needing to appear perfect; or of being afraid to be open and reaching out, depending on how you interpret it. Ask yourself the following questions:

- How angry do I get at little things, at insignificant behaviors of others?
- How upset do I become when I feel I failed in a minor interaction?
- How cold and withdrawn do I become if I strike out?
- How frustrated do I become when I can't control in life, when I can't pitch even though it is my ball?

- How often do I have to lie or exaggerate about my batting average in life?
- How uncomfortable do I feel with my false front?
- How many excuses do I have to make for my errors?

The degree to which you find yourself acting in these ways is a true index of the difficulty you experience in interpersonal interactions and a reflection of how much effort you must consciously exert to share yourself with others. All the more reason not to wait but to reach out this very day.

A short time ago a friend of mine described an incident that occurred on Mother's Day. She was having dinner with her parents and an aunt and uncle. Out of character for her, she began to relate an experience she had in her grandparents' home some years earlier. She had gone there with other members of the family because her grandfather was close to death. She was sleeping with her grandmother, whom she could hear puttering around her grandfather, making him comfortable and reassuring him quietly, almost in a whisper. She told her family that, as she heard the interaction between her grandparents, she almost cried with the realization of how much she loved her grandmother for the loving care and concern she demonstrated. With that her aunt broke into tears and pulled her close, as did her mother. Her father's eyes misted as he told her how much he loved her. For a moment there was closeness among them she had never before experienced. As I listened I could feel my own eyes tear up.

It's that simple. You need only honestly share your feelings, and love comes along. You can do it too, if you'll only try.

Index

142

Index

www.ingramcontent.com/pod-product-compliance
Lightning Source LLC
Chambersburg PA
CBHW070026300526

45794CB00001B/419